Supervising On The Line

A Self-Help Guide For First Line Supervisors

By Gene Gagnon

Published by Margo - Minnetonka, Minnesota

1st Edition

Copyright © 1987 by Gene Gagnon

Published by Margo
P.O. Box 1G
Minnetonka, MN 55345

Printed in the United States of America
First Margo Publications Printing: January 1988

Library of Congress Cataloging in Publication Data.
√ Gagnon, Gene, 1928-
Supervising On The Line
       √ 1. Supervision of employees.√ 2. Supervisors.
√ I. Title.
HF5549. 12. G34   1988   658.3'02   88-1673
ISBN 0-944671-00-4

This book is dedicated to all the first line supervisors I've worked with over the past 30 or so years who have taught me much more than I would ever be able to teach them.

Gene Gagnon

ACKNOWLEDGEMENTS

A book is a creation that involves a birthing process — it doesn't just happen. It is the result of many people's support along the way. Some of those deserve special acknowledgement.

Thank you first to my wife Marge, who always knew there was a book in there someplace.

To these people for their efforts; John Bush for his illustrations, Norine Larson and Caroline Anderson for editing and organization, and to my daughter Elizabeth Gagnon, for coordinating the project.

CONTENTS

Chapter 8 Continued

Push Button Power
Calling for Reinforcements
Different Strokes
Waiting for Mr. Right
Putting the Puzzle Together

FOREWORD

Much has been written on the subject of line supervision, but most such writings fail to hit the mark. Some of them tend to talk down to the reader, and they create the impression that the prime job of a supervisor is to make lots of lists and to get to work early. Others are the opposite — they are full of behavioral theory and academic folklore.

We were not surprised to see that Gene Gagnon has hit the bullseye and avoided the two extremes. Having had the pleasure of knowing and working with Gene for longer than either of us would care to admit, I have watched his viewpoint on warehousing change from that of a traditional industrial engineer to a behaviorist approach. As Gene has worked in an increasing variety of warehouses over the years, he has come to understand the fact that it is people, not machines, who make the difference between a good and a bad operation. This is especially true in warehouses, where close supervision is complicated by both the nature of the work and the physical factors involved in a large and busy distribution center.

Above all, Gene Gagnon's book is readable. It does not insult the intelligence of the reader, but his ideas are expressed in plain English, which is enhanced by attractive and potent illustrations. Line supervisors and their bosses are likely to use portions of this book as the basis of training sessions, as well as a handbook for ready reference as the problems of managing are faced on a day-to-day basis.

This book is a significant addition to the literature on warehouse management.

Kenneth B. Ackerman
President
The Ackerman Company
Columbus, OH

PREFACE

The foreman of a machinery department, a charge nurse in a hospital, the manager of accounts payable or the supervisor of receiving — all share the same responsibility. They are the first level of management. They are the first line supervisors.

The industries may be different but the jobs have a common base, they require dealing with people. To the employees they supervise these people represent the company. During my years as a consultant I have gained a great deal of respect for the people in these positions. I've seen that many times these supervisors are pulled between the workers and management, trying to satisfy the needs of both while still maintaining their own sanity. Their effectiveness, I've learned, depends on a variety of factors, including experience, training, self-esteem, confidence, leadership ability, communication skills and the backing of upper management.

In addition to these skills the first line supervisor in a warehouse has a unique problem. He can't usually observe all the people he supervises at any one time. They are scattered over many square feet of racks, stacks, trailers, boxcars, coolers, mezzanines and small rooms. Contrast this with a machinery department where a foreman can see with a glance whether or not his people are present at their stations; or the supervisor of a clerical department who can count "heads-up-heads down." How much easier it is to manage in those circumstances!

But a unique problem doesn't mean the situation is impossible. It just means special skills are needed. That's what this book is all about — to give the first line supervisor the tools he needs. It's impossible to put all the ideas from 30 years of learning into 131 pages, but this is an attempt to give you the most important ones. If you try some of them you will be a more effective supervisor-and you will like your job better. And when you do I'll feel I've done mine.

Gene Gagnon

CHAPTER 1

THE ROLE OF THE FIRST LINE SUPERVISOR

The Role Of The First Line Supervisor

Tony Mann bent his 6'1" frame to tighten the laces on his
steel-toed work boots and then straightened, rubbing the
tense muscles on one side of his neck. His first full week
as a supervisor had been a tough one. Standing on one of
the loading docks, Tony looked out over the Big Apple
warehouse where he'd worked for eleven years, the last
five of them as a forklift driver — one of the company's
best.

Tony remembered that when the warehouse manager
offered him the job as first line supervisor on the second
shift, he figured it would be a breeze. He knew the warehouse, and he knew the guys he'd be working with.
But after this past week, Tony wasn't quite so sure.

Although the crew worked hard for him, they still clocked
five straight days of overtime, and problems seemed end-
less. There were damaged goods, there were shorts, there
were unexpected deliveries and they got behind. They became frustrated, and then angry. By Friday night things got
so bad that Tony was sure two of the men were going to
strangle each other. To make matters worse, the manager
always seemed to show up just when all hell was breaking
loose. Tony knew the manager wasn't too happy with all
the overtime and delayed shipments, but what could a

rookie supervisor do about it, anyway?

Entering the Twilight Zone

Tony made it through that first week, but he had to admit
that the job was no picnic. Actually, Tony didn't know
what he was doing. He had thought that supervising would
be rewarding, but his experience so far had been nothing
but frustration and anxiety. He didn't feel good about
ordering his friends around, he didn't think they liked it
either. He began to think that he had passed through a
Twilight Zone and now he was someone else—someone
who wasn't completely trusted by either the crew or the
warehouse manager. He wondered if the guys thought he
was a little stiff because of his new title. Did he act like
their boss? Was he too demanding? Not demanding
enough? He couldn't figure it out. Then he talked to a
veteran supervisor on another shift. Tony discovered he
wasn't the only one who felt strange and uncomfortable in
the new role of first line supervisor.

More Than Running a Forklift

Tony's predicament is a familiar one. I've seen it in
countless warehouses. New first line supervisors are
yanked from the ranks on Friday, and when they return to
work on Monday they're wearing shirts and ties. They've
emptied their lockers and left their lunch pails at home.
Like most new first line supervisors, Tony Mann received a
handsome promotion but little or no training. He's run a

forklift for years, and he knows what everyone in the Big Apple warehouse does, but he hasn't learned how to manage people. With one week of on-the-job experience behind him, Tony understands his new job a little more than he did at the start. Tony was lucky, he got some help from another supervisor.

I believe the first line supervisor cannot learn his job on-the-job, unless he's either real lucky or a born leader. He can't pick up tips as the months go by and weld them together into a productive management style. The warehouse business is too demanding, too fast-paced, too full of changes and surprises. The new first line supervisor needs and deserves help the minute he gets on the job.

If **you're a new supervisor,** like Tony Mann is, **or a frustrated veteran, this book is for you.** Whether you work in a public or private warehouse, **your job depends on efficiency, productivity, and service.** Keeping costs low and performance high is not only the warehouse manager's ball game. The first line supervisor must plan too, because he is directly responsible for his employees' productivity.

The High-Priced Asset

Not long ago, businesses considered the storage and distribution of goods a necessary evil. Production and sales were considered the two most important functions in the manufacturing process. Workers made the product, and the

sales force sold it. But business people overlooked the important steps between A and B, between completion of the finished product and the moment it reaches the customer. Today, ignoring the price of storing and transporting goods can be expensive. Distribution accounts for nearly one-quarter of a product's total cost — that's about $8 on a pair of work boots.

Just as retailers and producers realize they can't take storage and distribution for granted, **the first line supervisor can no longer underestimate the importance of his job.** He's the person who makes it all work. Warehousing is an expensive, labor-intensive industry. Employees are not listed on the company balance sheet, but **people are the most valuable, high-priced asset in the warehouse.** And, who manages this costly asset? The first line supervisor! Compare the price tag of wages and benefits for a ten-man crew with the cost of a forklift and you'll see the heavy investment a company makes in human-power. If those ten people each earn $30,000 a year (including benefits), the supervisor is responsible for a $300,000 asset.

To illustrate the cost of labor, let's show how five minutes wasted here and there can add up to thousands of wasted dollars. If the crew punches in at 8:00 a.m., how often are they filling orders at 8:01? Chances are they lost ten minutes before start-up. And when break-time comes, twice during the shift, the workers probably leave five minutes early or return to their machines five minutes late. If they are allowed 30 minutes for lunch, how many operators shave an extra five minutes before and after? Do they start packing up ten minutes before quitting time?

I've seen this happen repeatedly in warehouses and neither the supervisors nor management realize how much it actually costs. If a worker loses 45 minutes in this way that's almost ten percent of his total day. Multiply that same ten percent by $300,000 annual salary paid a crew of ten, and those lost minutes represent a yearly loss of $30,000 for the warehouse.

The Real Thing

Storing and shipping goods, as I've said, isn't cheap. As the costs rise and the competition gets more intense, the warehouse industry changes. The role of the first line supervisor follows suit. Date-coding, computerized inventory systems and government regulations affect everything from the warehouse layout and loading schedules to the number of workers needed. Outside forces shape your job, too. Consider what happened at Coca-Cola for example. Once upon a time, there was one kind of Coke for everyone all over the world. It bore no other name than Coke, and maybe a catchy slogan. That was it. Today, however, there are at least six different flavors of Coke, including diet, caffeine-free and cherry.

Many other consumer products are expanding in number like Coke, and every one of them requires not only extra shelf space in the supermarket, but additional cubic feet and pick slots on the warehouse floor. Another trend typical of the changes affecting warehousing operations is the spread of those small convenience stores that seem to spring up overnight. These street-corner shops, open all hours and usually hooked up to gas pumps, need more frequent deliveries of smaller orders.

The Key to the Warehouse

Don't let anyone fool you, **your job as a first line supervisor is critical to the warehouse industry.** It may be hectic, you may get frazzled, and you may or may not end up behind a big desk in an air-conditioned office, but believe me, **your job is just as important as any in top management.**

Compare the warehouse with the military for a minute, and think of the difference between soldiers on the battlefield and those in the rear area. Soldiers on the front line earn a different set of stripes than those behind the lines. Both jobs are important, but everyone knows which group shoulders the brunt of the attack. As every first line supervisor knows, the warehouse can be a battlefield, with the supervisor on the firing line.

In some operations, the supervisor is called the <u>front line</u> supervisor. First line supervisors may fight it out in the trenches, but neither management nor the supervisors themselves seem to realize the importance of the first line job. I think **supervisors should be considered part of management, because that's what they do: manage the**

human resources that run the warehouse. The first line supervisor may not have much decision-making power when it comes to purchasing new equipment, or even hiring employees, but he <u>does</u> control the productivity of the warehouse. And that, after all, determines whether the balance sheet is red or black.

Fighting Fire With Fire

First line supervisors need to manage themselves before they can hope to run a productive crew. I've seen too many first-class supervisors frustrated with their jobs because they spend all their time fending off one crisis after another, bogging themselves down. That happened with one young supervisor I met who had an idea for rearranging the layout of his warehouse section to prevent shorts. Although he knew a better way to organize the place, he grew disillusioned because he didn't have enough time or energy to do it. Like Tony Mann, he felt like he spent all his time fighting fires, filling unscheduled shipments, dealing with the shorts, working overtime every night, instead of doing his real job. It's tough to remember the purpose of your trip through the swamp when you're up to your rear end in alligators. Reactive management robs both the first line supervisor and the employee of productive, satisfying work. Supervisors need to take control of their warehouse, to plan work and act <u>before</u> minor problems become crises.

Being an active manager also involves setting goals for

9

WAREHOUSING
SWAMP

yourself and your employees. Some people think goal is a four letter word. I don't agree that goals are unnatural or forced. I think that people want and need goals. Everyone has worked with goals in some form since grade school, from getting good report cards and high test scores to making the varsity basketball team. Every sport revolves around setting and achieving goals. Without them, there would be no object to the game, no rules or winning scores. Just as a coach explains the game plan to his players, an active supervisor sets goals for his employees and lets them know exactly what's expected of them. You don't enjoy working in a vacuum, not knowing what's expected, and I'll bet your employees don't either.

Building A Positive Work Environment

While the first line supervisor may have been promoted for being a good forklift driver, like Tony Mann, he now has to motivate others to do the job. **The first line supervisor's performance now depends on his work crew's productivity.** When you are accustomed to doing things yourself, it is not always easy to start relying on others to do the job for you. It's enough to make a supervisor nervous. When he gets anxious, a supervisor is more likely to watch his employees like a hawk, assuming they are a bunch of goldbricks. A lot of folks think that people are naturally lazy, but after spending more than 30 years working within various warehouses, I'm convinced that most people want to do a good job.

Not only do they want to do a good job, but workers today are smarter, more sophisticated and more willing to plan an active role in their work. **That's why a supervisor needs to be less of the traditional boss** — one who looks over an employee's shoulder, and fights to get the work done — **and more of a coach.** A supervisor who tries to ramrod orders is working against his employees, not with them. That only causes resentment. First line supervisors can accomplish more by helping employees, removing the barriers that prevent them from doing their best. That's what I call creating a **positive work environment.**

In an environment like that, people work hard, not because they're afraid for their jobs, but because they believe they can make a difference. It's up to you to convince your workers that you care about them and the quality of their work, and that the company does too. One of the most effective ways of creating a positive environment is by listening to your operators, and acting on what they tell you. Nothing destroys an employee's motivation faster than the feeling that **no one cares** how he does his job.

"They Don't Care"

I ran into this kind of negative attitude in a warehouse where order selection had just switched from a tow line to double pallet jacks. While I was out on the floor, I stopped one of the operators and asked him how he liked the double pallets.

"Don't like them — they're different!" he said. "Besides, you engineers aren't so smart — I can <u>walk</u> faster than this new jack can pull itself."

Well, that sent up a warning sign. I knew the jacks were supposed to move faster than that. "Have you told your supervisor?" I asked.

"Nah, why tell him? He wouldn't do anything about it anyway. Doesn't do any good to talk to the management around here."

I reported what the operator had said to the warehouse manager. A little research showed that the pallet jacks had been set wrong at the factory and were running 20 percent slower than they should have been. No one on the floor had bothered to mention it. They figured management didn't care.

Is that the sort of message you're sending your employees?

I believe it's part of the first line supervisor's basic responsibility to get out on the floor and <u>listen</u> to his employees. Think of the supervisor's role as a magnifying glass. The employees view the company through you. In most warehouses, workers seldom see the warehouse manager, much less the company president. That's why you, the first line supervisor, have the ability to shape the way employees feel about their job and the company. And, if you believe — as I do — that people, who feel good about the job they do, are more productive, you can make the work environment a positive one.

More Than A Screwdriver

Don't get me wrong, I'm not telling you to coddle or pamper your workers. Helping employees do their best isn't even a matter of being nice. It's a matter of good sense. If they grow more productive, your job becomes less frustrating and more secure. To build a positive work environment, a supervisor needs skills — tools he can grab and use. If you tell a car mechanic to fix your carburetor, but only provide him with a screwdriver, you're asking for trouble. In the same way, **a supervisor needs the right tools for the job: time management and communication skills, authority and responsibility, feedback and information.** Think of this book as a tool box containing the information every supervisor needs to help himself and those around him.

Tony Mann, the new supervisor I've described here, didn't have the tools he needed to do his job. Tony had a right to expect the information, training and authority he needed to do the job properly. When you're in charge of loading 14 trucks with a crew that's short two workers, you don't have time to look through a manual or hunt down another supervisor for advice. And, you don't need a manager who takes credit for the successes and blames you for the failures. **A first line supervisor, whether he's a rookie or a veteran, has the right to expect the same sort of support from**

management that he gives his employees. That includes goals, clearly defined responsibilities and open communication.

Sure, this book presents an ideal picture of the role of the supervisor, and not everyone works in a situation they can readily change. Maybe it'll just make you more frustrated with your position. But the following chapters can fill in the blanks, providing the sort of information you need to help you through the supervising Twilight Zone. If you can use any part of this book to help you make your job more rewarding and those who work for you more productive, what have you got to lose?

CHAPTER 2

RESPONSIBILITY, ACCOUNTABILITY AND AUTHORITY

MANAGEMENT

WORKERS

SUPERVISORY ZONE

Responsibility, Accountability and Authority

Out On A Limb

It had been a long hot summer for Gary Simmons since his manager promoted him to first line supervisor on the new night shift. Gary thought that he had learned the ropes as fast as anyone, though he had only one day of formal training. He got on well with the crew, with the exception of Bob Wenzel, one of the order pickers, who seemed to ooze a bad attitude. Gary found himself frustrated by Bob's marginal work habits.

One morning, after leaving a hectic scheduling session, Gary spied Bob sauntering into the warehouse more than 20 minutes late for his shift. Without really thinking about it, Gary decided to show Bob that he meant business. Catching up to the worker near the order desk, Gary tapped Bob's sleeve with his clipboard.

"Hey Bob!" Gary said, "Is getting to work on time too much trouble for you this week? You've been late more than once, you know."

"Looks like I didn't miss much," the order picker grinned. "Besides, my watch hasn't been working lately."

"That's a good one!" Gary snorted. "Why don't you just take the rest of the day off?"

Bob muttered something before stomping out, but Gary felt good about the way he'd handled the situation. "A supervisor has to be decisive," he told himself, "and let people know who's boss."

Doing it by the Book

Gary didn't notice that Bob stopped to talk with the union's representative on his way out. Later that day Rob Ward, the warehouse manager, called Gary into his office. When he arrived, Gary noticed that the union representative was there, and he wasn't smiling.

"Gary, what the devil were you thinking when you told Bob Wenzel to go home this morning? Don't you realize we have to operate under the rules of the union contract?" Rob said, scowling.

The union representative nodded. "In case you don't remember, Mr. First Line Supervisor, the contract requires you to document two verbal and one written warning for an employee's file before suspending him. As far as we can see," he added, "you didn't give any warnings or keep any records."

Unfortunately for Gary, the union representative was right. Bob knew the contract better than Gary did. That's why he reported the action to the union representative before going home.

"You're lucky, Gary!" the manager said. "The union isn't going to make a big issue out of this one. Still," he added, glancing at the union representative, "I think it would be better if you patched it up with Wenzel."

Gary Simmons gritted his teeth and nodded. "Great", he thought, by now the whole crew knew about his mess-up. He had tried to speak softly and carry a big stick on the warehouse floor, but it looked like Rob Ward had just taken the stick away. Gary didn't understand why the whole episode with Bob Wenzel was such a big deal.

Feeling as if management had sacrificed him to the union, Gary decided that if the company didn't mind employees coming to work late, he wasn't going to put his neck on the line either.

Using a Different Set of Tools

This situation should never have happened. It happened because Gary didn't understand that part of his job was studying the union contract, — before he ever thought of sending Bob home for the day. It happened because the company did not train Gary in the correct disciplinary procedure. It happened because Gary and his boss did not define the responsibilities of the first line supervisor's job.

A supervisor like Gary, who doesn't understand his job, is

out on a limb. And, if his manager doesn't provide the information the supervisor needs to make good decisions, he's sawing off the branch that supports the supervisor.

When a warehouse worker gets promoted to first line supervisor, he leaves behind the physical tools that go with his job — the forklift, the pallet jack, the dock plate. The supervisor no longer needs to move cases, he needs to motivate people and move products. He needs different tools. **Job definition is the first tool that a supervisor can use to gain more satisfaction from his work.** He can better define his first line position by understanding three key elements: **Responsibility, Accountability and Authority.**

These elements won't be found in a standard job description. Most job descriptions tend to list a set of tasks, but a first line supervisor needs to know more than his basic duties. Consider a football team. While it's important for the coach and his players to learn their field positions, that doesn't make them a team. Anybody who knows the positions can play the game. In order to build a winning team, however, everyone needs to know the play book.

Responsibility: The What and the Why

Although running a warehouse is no game, there are some similarities. A football player had better know exactly what's expected of him before he gets on the field, because the play book assumes that everyone knows his position.

The book describes the plays each player is responsible for, — the moves that ultimately make or break a team. It's the same for a first line supervisor. Unless he understands management's objectives, the overall game plan, he can't do a good job. That's why I think of responsibility as the "what" and "why" of a job.

Whether you understand them or not, the rules run the game. Every supervisor has objectives laid out for him, just as he places similar expectations on his employees. Gary unknowingly broke some of the rules and he paid the price. Don't let this happen to you. Find out exactly what management expects. **That's what responsibility is all about; understanding expectations, learning the game plan.**

Heading in the Right Direction

If you planned to meet a friend at the airport, you would most likely choose a meeting place. If not, where would you go first? The ticket counter? The baggage terminal? The gate? Agreeing on job objectives may seem as obvious as choosing a rendezvous, but it often gets overlooked when managers and supervisors sit down to talk, — if they ever do. Although they're in the same building, neither has told the other exactly where they are, or where they're going. In fact, any correlation between how a supervisor and his boss perceive the first line job is often purely coincidental. Does this sound familiar? **Meeting with**

your boss to define your job is one of the most basic and important steps you can take in becoming an effective supervisor.

Approaching your boss to ask for a more detailed account of your responsibilities may not sound realistic. Some people don't agree with me when I say that first line supervisors are managers, and refuse to accept the ideas in this book. I know, they've told me so! If you feel that your manager won't be very helpful, that gives you more reason to be assertive and take an active role in defining your job. This is something you have to do for yourself. When you're driving a car that's skidding down an icy road, you have two options: one is to turn the steering wheel in the direction of the skid while pumping the brakes; the other to give up and hit the ditch or another car.

I've seen a lot of warehouse supervisors, including 20-year veterans, who have given up. Supervisors like these are just going with the flow, preparing to hit the ditch. Although they have great potential, these supervisors feel that the job is out of their control. If you feel like this, don't get discouraged. Instead, make a list of your responsibilities and give it to your manager. For example, you may feel that your responsibilities include distributing work, preparing reports, resolving grievances and training new employees. Review the list with your manager and he'll have something to react to. This way you can discover the parameters of your job before finding yourself on a patch of ice, like Gary Simmons.

Accountability: Knowing the Score

Responsibility usually doesn't alter much over time. It may always be the supervisor's responsibility to increase productivity, improve customer service, or reduce damages, but he'll take different steps to meet those objectives from year to year. Those steps are what I call accountability. Whether you're taking a road trip or watching a football game, there are definite markers to tell you what's going on. On the road, there are signs and mileage markers; on the football field, it's scoreboards and yardlines. While responsibility involves the "big-picture", part of a supervisor's job accountability deals with specific, short-term goals that fulfill those objectives.

Unlike responsibility, accountability changes with time as priorities shift. I remember one grocery warehouse that was temporarily shut down by the Food and Drug Administration (FDA) because the warehouse flunked the sanitation inspection. You can bet nothing was more important than improving sanitary conditions for the next six months, because the government was watching that warehouse like a hawk. The first line supervisors were held accountable for using a checklist of 60 housekeeping criteria. Their goal: to have less than three items marked against the warehouse. During those six months, sanitation and housekeeping took priority over shortages, overtime, and increasing throughput.

Accountability is the measurement of a supervisor's progress toward meeting management's objectives. For some time now, Management By Objectives has been a popular strategy for setting specific goals and measuring progress in an organization. As a first line supervisor, you may not feel connected with company goals, but they affect your job, just as you can affect your company's success in achieving them. Control your job, don't let it control you. You can take ownership of your work by applying the company's objectives to your own work. For example, one long-term objective might involve improving warehouse security; a dock supervisor would then be accountable for inspecting and locking the loading docks after his shift. The supervisor needs to know how that goal applies to his area, and exactly what "improving security" means; whether it's zero doors left open during the month, or less than five doors.

A goal means nothing unless it's based on zero. Let's say that a shift crew averages 250,000 cases throughput a month, and the manager tells the supervisor that he should move more product the next month. That means very little; 250,001 is more. A first line supervisor who operates without learning the exact goal could go for a month, or a year, thinking he's doing great by increasing throughput one percent, while management has been expecting a 10 percent increase. **It's crucial for supervisors to get frequent, accurate feedback from their managers, even if they have to ask for it.** Having an accurate picture of the accountability of your job is like knowing the score of

the game. Fans expect to learn whether a favorite team
won or lost, game by game, not at the end of the season.
Unfortunately, many supervisors don't learn management's
objectives until their performance review. A supervisor
and his employees, like sports fans, need to know how
things stand from week to week, not after six months.

Authority: Taking Control

When Gary Simmons suspended Bob Wenzel, he thought
he was doing a good job. But, Gary understood neither the
company's disciplinary procedure nor the limits of his
authority. If you've been in a situation in which a manager
overrules your decision, or end-runs you to deal directly
with your employees, you know it's not a good feeling.

A first line supervisor has to take the first step when it
comes to defining his job. Clarify the limits of your
authority before you find yourself out on a limb; make sure
that you have the authority and support to fulfill the responsibilities and goals established by management. You have
to understand your authority before you can use it effectively.

When I managed a manufacturing group, one of the training sessions we held for the first line supervisors involved a
mock arbitration session. The company's labor attorney
played the arbitrator, while two supervisors represented the
union and two represented the company. One of the men
playing the union role had been a steward in the past, and

so he knew the contract thoroughly. His team got exactly what they wanted and cut the company representatives apart. The other team, however, was in a difficult position because the members were unfamiliar with the contract in regards to the company's rights and their decision-making powers.

Be An Authority Figure

It pays to know the scope of the authority given you by management. Failing to use the power you have can cause just as many problems as overstepping your authority. There is no single, right leadership style, but a supervisor does need to be <u>some</u> kind of leader. Taking charge generates the organized environment that I believe employees want to work in; most people dislike chaos. The supervisor can provide the leadership that builds the best possible working atmosphere for employees. I've met many supervisors who don't realize what a big difference they can make in the warehouse. As a first line supervisor, you need confidence in your own authority, plus confidence that management will back you up.

Furthermore, I would like to see supervisors use their authority to gain a greater say in hiring decisions. The supervisor should see a new employee for the first time at an interview, not on the day he starts. As long as the supervisor is held accountable for his employees' performance, it seems only right that he has a say in getting his people. Then too, employees show greater ownership in the quality of their work when the person who hired them is standing nearby, rather than in an office upstairs.

Taking the Bull by the Horns ...

While there's only so much one supervisor can do, he <u>can</u> do a lot. **And that is one of the keys to defining the first line supervisor's job; knowing the boundaries.** If you're uncertain about how much authority or responsibility comes with the job, it's better to find out now. Once you cross the line, you may be lost. I want to help you map out your job so that you know where you stand.

One of the job's boundaries that seems especially mudded is the supervisor's span of control. I've been in many warehouses where supervisors are responsible for crews of 20, even 40 employees. To me, that's not managing, that's herding. A football team has 11 players on the field, not 15 or 20. Similarly, there should be a limit to the number of employees assigned to a first line supervisor.

Overseeing so many employees takes valuable time away from the first line supervisor; time that could be spent scheduling work, solving problems, or communicating. Even if a supervisor is effective, trying to keep track of 20 people in a warehouse will waste time, therefore money, for the operation. Management could pay the salary of another first line supervisor with the savings it realized in improved employee productivity. If you oversee more than 12 people, it may be time for you to sit down with your boss and come to some understanding about your role in the warehouse.

I know that a lot of first line supervisors feel that they're not getting the support they deserve from management. In many cases this is true, but I believe **you have to take the bull by the horns and go after what you need to make your job more rewarding.** Management may not rush order the information and guidelines for your job, so it's up to you to ask for it. Not everyone agrees with me, I know, but your boss may even be relieved when he realizes you are taking ownership in your job by asking for a clear definition.

... And the Elephant by the Ears

Sometimes the process of defining a first line supervisor's job reminds me of the old story about the blind men describing an elephant. One grabbed the trunk and said the animal resembled a snake; another circled a leg with his arms and declared it a tree trunk; while the third man felt an ear and reported that the elephant was really more like a flapping tent.

Although each of the men perceived a part of the elephant, none of them put the pieces together to come up with an accurate picture. In the same way, supervisors may be seeing only part of their job. I've discussed three areas of the first line supervisor's job in this chapter. Understanding only one or two would be like describing an elephant as all trunk or all ears. You need all three—responsibility, accountability, and authority—to get the true picture.

CHAPTER 3

MANAGING TIME AND SOLVING PROBLEMS

Managing Time And Solving Problems

For five years, Mike Miller worked summers and holidays as a vacation replacement for Faber Foods warehouse while taking classes at City College. When Mike finished school, Red Manning, the night superintendent, hired him as a dock coordinator in the produce department. But Mike wasn't long for the dock. Six months later, a supervisor's slot opened up, and Mike Miller applied for the job. He became one of Faber's youngest first line supervisors.

Mike left City College with a management degree and a healthy dose of idealism. He hoped to put some of his textbook skills into practice for Faber's warehouse. While he worked part-time on the dock, however, Mike was getting only a partial picture of what it really took to run a warehouse shift.

Out of the Frying Pan, Into the Fire

Now, 16 months after becoming a first line supervisor, Mike Miller barely managed to finish his work in 12 hours. The feeling that he knew better ways to manage his crew, but didn't have time to put those ideas into practice, was the most frustrating part of Mike's job. He was one of two supervisors working five nights in the grocery department, and together they had about 45 employees reporting to them.

Mike handled labor scheduling, which included assigning

the part-time employees and replenishing stock. Red
Manning left his job as superintendent and the position
went unfilled for two months. During that time, Mike
stopped getting the performance reports he had used for
scheduling. Without that information, he had no way to
chart the productivity of his employees. Tracking down
shortages was by far the most time-consuming part of his
job. Every night, it seemed that more and more products
were slotted wrong. Mike knew that Faber's problem with
shorts could easily be solved by keeping better grocery
inventory records, or re-slotting the products, but he felt too
preoccupied with minute-to-minute crises to do anything
about it.

It Takes More Than Excedrin

Being a first line supervisor was getting to be a headache
for Mike — a migraine headache. Like a lot of people,
however, Mike was treating his headache with aspirin,
without finding the pain's source. Whenever he found
another problem in the warehouse, or felt himself falling
behind, Mike would spend more time at work, which
essentially meant taking a couple more aspirin. But no
matter how much time he spent at it, he could never catch
up, much less get ahead.

**Too often we treat the symptoms, not the source, of our
problems.** I once had a headache that lasted for weeks,
even after feeding it daily doses of aspirin. After two
weeks of pain I finally went to the dentist and discovered

35

that the real problem was an impacted tooth.

It's much the same for first line supervisors like Mike. Although there didn't seem to be enough hours in the day for him to complete all his work, that was only a symptom of other, larger problems: supervising too many employees, lacking the information necessary to schedule his work crew, mis-slotted products. Those were the "impacted teeth" of Mike's job that devoured the time he could have spent improving his crew's productivity or installing more effective work scheduling programs.

Like a lot of other first line supervisors, Mike was caught up in a cycle of reacting to problems instead of solving them. In the same way, no amount of aspirin would cure my headache until the dentist pulled the impacted tooth. Supervisors must also find and solve the roots of their problems, or they will continue to see the same ones returning to haunt them.

Several years ago, one of our client companies reported that they were having trouble with high indirect labor costs. After spending some time observing what was happening on the floor, the problem became clear.

"You're losing time through equipment breakdowns," I reported to the company president.

"What? Has that one come around the block again?" he

scoffed. "I thought we solved that problem when we brought in that outside maintenance company to repair all the forklifts and pallet jacks."

The president's response made it clear that he had been treating his headaches with aspirin. A "one time fix" did not solve the real cause of the problem. What he needed was an ongoing preventive maintenance program to keep their equipment in top shape.

I think **first line supervisors should consider their job a type of preventive maintenance.** Remove the source of potential problems before they grow, and you'll have more time to do your job. A preventive maintenance schedule for machines provides a schedule for tune-ups, engine adjustments, and part replacements. Time management would do the same for first line supervisors. Time management is active management. Mike Miller was burning out on his job, spending more time fighting fires than supervising. Reeling from crisis to crisis takes a lot of energy, and leaves supervisors feeling less and less in control.

Fire fighting is not only frustrating, it's expensive. In the board game Monopoly, players get a certain amount of money at the game's start. If they spend half of it on fines, rents and taxes, they probably won't have enough left to buy property or hotels. Time, like Monopoly money, is a finite resource, and should be used wisely. Unlike Monopoly, managing that resource doesn't depend on the roll of the dice. Supervisors have a choice.

At the same time, the money lost through poor time management isn't play money. **When a first line supervisor spends more time fighting fires than supervising his employees, the effectiveness of the whole group decreases.** Productivity could easily drop ten percent. For a work crew of ten, that ten percent decline is equivalent to one employee's salary—as much as $30,000 a year wasted. In Mike Miller's case, with 45 employees, lost productivity could cost Faber Foods as much as $135,000 annually.

Starting at Home

If you are a first line supervisor and you feel that you're losing the battle to get everything in a so-so style, you need to regain control. There are two aspects of time management: managing your own time, and managing your employees' time. The place to start is with your time. From the first chapter of this book I've been talking about several tools that would help you become a better first line supervisor. I believe the **key to effective management is better time management, and that means planning, prioritizing, scheduling.** Determining how your time is spent, and comparing it with how it should be spent, can help you identify and quantify the problems that consume your work day.

There's an old industrial engineering technique called work sampling that you can use to get a grip on your time. Work sampling involves keeping a daily time log to track your day. Choose a couple of days each month at random.

Every half hour list what you have done, including any
events or problems that required your attention during that
time.

Keeping a log can underscore the difference between how
you think you're spending your time, and how you're
actually spending it. I know of a company where the
warehouse manager, wondering where his time went, kept a
log of his activitities. He was surprised to learn that he had
spent 60 percent of his time one week working on grievances. The manager's limited time was only the headache.
The log highlighted his real problem, — the large number
of grievances.

Priorities: Get Them Straight

Once you know where your time is going, you can throw
away the aspirin and start curing the source of your headaches. The time log can show you where your time is
going, but only you know how it should be spent. In the
last chapter, I talked about the importance of knowing your
job, and understanding your responsibility, accountability
and authority. This is where that knowledge gets useful.
**The better you know your objectives, the better you'll
be able to channel energy in the right direction.**

List your short and long-term objectives. Which of them
are most important to your job? If you tried to put an equal
amount of energy into all your goals, they would over-
whelm you. Establishing priorities is a tool that focuses

attention on important tasks. And it's as simple as A, B, C. Label each of your objectives with an A, B, or C, in order of their importance. Identify your "A" tasks and do something about them. Update the list regularly, re-examining the value of your activities. The A , B, C labels aren't written in stone. Today's A's may become tomorrow's C's. Keep an eye on your priorities. The most time-consuming tasks are often the least vital ones. Make sure the time you spend on tasks is relative to their importance.

You can use the list of priorities to plan your day, and to evaluate your performance. By following a plan, you're not just doing something for the sake of being busy. Stick to one task at a time, doing the most important thing now. The check marks next to the tasks on your list will measure your progress toward meeting your objectives.

The Flip Side of the Coin

Planning and scheduling are two sides of the same coin. You have gathered information on your time habits, examined and prioritized your goals. Now you're ready to plug that information into a schedule for your employees.

Planning is a good investment. I'd be willing to bet that every hour spent planning saves the first line supervisor three or four hours on the job. Try to plan for each day the night before: jot down shipments that will be arriving, orders that must be filled, how much time each task is allotted, who will be working. Don't forget to schedule in

some time for the unexpected events that can ruin an inflexible plan. No matter how sketchy it is, this list will give your work day some order.

Scheduling, even if it's only four hours in advance, will also put order into your employee's day. Work shouldn't just "happen." If the first line supervisor doesn't schedule, the employees often will do it themselves. In warehousing, it's all too easy for operators to develop their own system of methods and schedules. In almost every operation involving humans, there will be some lost time. The purpose of scheduling is to keep that loss to a minimum.

Types of Time

There are two types of lost time: obvious and hidden. Obvious lost time is exactly what it means. A forklift operator leaning against his machine with nothing to do, or an order selector with no orders to pick. Hidden lost time, however, is spent on problems within operations.

One of our clients was amazed to find out how much time the company lost at the beginning of each shift because work was not scheduled and waiting for the crew. Every morning, 15 employees surrounded the first line supervisor to get their orders. Then they had to round up equipment and pallets before actually getting down to productive work. Management estimated that the time lost every morning in that warehouse carried a price tag of more than $60,000 a year.

Does this sound familiar? If the shift starts at 7 a.m., how many of your employees are actually working on an order at 7:10? Our client solved the problem by having someone from maintenance arrive half an hour before the shift began to prepare everything for the first orders of the day. This person would check the forklift batteries and line up the jacks with a pallet on each one, for example. The first line supervisor reduced the first-order bottleneck by scheduling the day well in advance, so that there were orders waiting for each operator.

Hidden lost time accounts for about 80 percent of lost time, yet attracts only 20 percent of management's problem-solving attention. Scheduling focuses attention on hidden lost time and highlights problems. **By scheduling, a first line supervisor places an expectation on each task.** If the job takes more time, it's a signal for the supervisor to look closer for a possible problem with methods or the system.

One particular situation comes to mind when I think of hidden lost time. A rail car full of bicycles arrived at one warehouse. The first line supervisor told me "It usually takes us three hours to unload bicycles." According to my standard, they should have finished the job in about an hour and a half. I decided to watch this operation. Their method involved a crew of three men, two working in the car placing bicycles on pallets, and a forklift driver who picked up the pallets and put them into storage.

I noticed that after the employees unloading the car pallet-ized the bicycles, they had to wait for the forklift to return. As it turned out, the forklift driver was losing time search-ing for empty slots to store the pallets. The receiving supervisor developed a two-step method to prevent the lost time: calculate the number of pallets required by the load and then locate enough empty slots for them. A simple solution, but it made a difference of more than one hour.

Once you discover the problems causing hidden lost time, they're often easy to remedy. One public warehouse was having a lot of trouble with congested loading docks be-cause the supervisor didn't have an effective scheduling system. The shipping crew would have orders for different trucks leaving around the same time, so they sorted the loads for each truck in advance. When the trucks pulled up to the dock however, there was confusion over which pallet stack belonged to which truck. The company solved this bottleneck by simply painting and numbering lanes. Using the numbers, the shipping department designated each truck to a lane and the loading crews knew where to place the pallets.

Life in the Fast Lane

Life in the warehouse travels at a frantic pace, but there are certain work patterns that the first line supervisor can use to schedule the day. The trick is to find the information you need. Sometimes the information comes from observation,

— keeping track of the time needed to unload bicycles, for example. Don't always depend on tradition however, because there's usually a great deal of hidden lost time built into old methods. Assume that the information you need to plan and schedule is available somewhere. Try looking in other departments like data processing, payroll or cost accounting.

The receiving room manager for a discount store was frustrated because delivery trucks often arrived unexpectedly, catching him unprepared. Unloading the truck required four extra people, and it was difficult for the manager to schedule them when he was unsure of the delivery time. Either he paid the workers for waiting, or scrambled for help when the truck arrived. The information was available for the manager's asking. The warehouse that sent the trucks knew when they were scheduled to arrive at the store, and what was on them. A phone call from the warehouse, giving the receiving room manager at least a day's warning of a delivery, solved the problem.

Although life in the warehouse is usually hectic, there are sometimes lulls that you can use to complete odd jobs that might otherwise fall by the wayside. Carry a notebook — I call it a traveling "job jar" — in your pocket so you can jot down these one-time tasks. That way you'll be ready when one of your employees has nothing to do. Some ideas for your job jar: looking for empty slots, counting products, sorting or fixing pallets, housekeeping, re-numbering aisles and re-packing damaged products.

The Gumshoe of the Warehouse

In a way, managing your time is like being a private detective. You have to be observant to find the hidden lost time in your own work and the work of your employees. You have to look for patterns, or "modus operandi," that can help you schedule. And you have to gather the information you need to plan. According to Parkinson's Law, work expands to fill the time allowed. Time management can make the first line supervisor's job more manageable by preventing his work from expanding unnecessarily.

CHAPTER 4

MEASUREMENT

Measurement

In the previous chapter, I urged first line supervisors to set and prioritize their objectives. But, what good are objectives if you have no way to measure your progress toward those objectives? There's an old slogan I like that says, "If you can't measure it, you can't manage it." Measurement is a tool that the first line supervisor can use to build a more positive work environment.

About fifteen years ago, a young man took his first job as an engineer with an Iowa turkey processing plant. Back then, turkey was primarily still a holiday dish. The processing was done between July and December. The employees were busy during those months, but the plant's managers had no way of tracking employee performance, or even the productivity of the plant. Although company officials were skeptical, the young engineer set about developing a system for measuring the plant's output.

Measuring the plant's output wasn't as easy as it had seemed at first. Unlike cars, toothbrushes or other products that have a unit price (and are units in themselves), the turkeys were packaged individually, but sold per pound. So while the company measured its sales in dollars or pounds, the employees spent their time handling individual birds. And those individual birds were not all the same. Processing time took about fifteen percent longer for the largest birds.

I was that young engineer challenged by this problem. The experience taught me a lesson I'll always remember.

I worked in the plant's cold, damp, shipping room along with nearly forty-five people, most of them women wearing gloves to keep their hands from turning into prunes. The birds came down a hanging conveyor, ready for packaging after being chilled to fifty degrees. The shipping room employees took the birds off the conveyor hanger, stuffed them with the neck and giblets, and bagged them, sealing them with a clamp.

I figured that the most accurate way to measure the output of the plant was to count the birds processed. But management disagreed with every method I suggested. "We could use a wand on the conveyor," I said. "Nah, wands won't work!" "Well then," I asked, "how about an electric eye?" "Nope! The dampness will short out the system!" It was clear they had convinced themselves they couldn't measure the plant's output. It was also quite evident that they would not tolerate a contrary opinion.

Frustrated, I went back to the drawing board — in this case, the shipping room — to observe the whole operation one more time. That was the day I noticed the lady who stood at the head of the conveyor line. She paused in her work and walked to the doorway leading into the lunchroom. There was a row of metal tags hanging from a wire over the door, and she moved one of them over to the opposite side,

51

abacus style.

"What are you doing?" I asked.

"See that broken hook in the conveyor?" She answered. "There are three hundred hooks in the line and whenever that one comes by about three hundred birds have been removed. So each of these tags over the door represents 300 turkeys. We like to do 12,000 birds a day for the company. When people take their break, they can count the tags to see how well we're doing."

So while managers and engineers debated the merit of measuring output, the employees had already established a daily goal and were keeping track of their own performance. They wanted to know how they were doing, even if the company did not. This experience convinced me that people want to feel good about their work. They want to go home knowing that they did a good job. When I reported the employees' method to the packaging room supervisor, he was surprised, and a little miffed.

From Widgets to Warehouse

Time and time again, I have visited warehouses where management says, "We don't have any measurement or standards." Then I'll go out on the floor where the operator says, "We do 100 of these an hour." Or the first line supervisor pulls a notebook out of his back pocket, looks up a particular shipment and says, "We usually finish that one in two hours." Like the turkey processing plant, workers often set up informal standards in the warehouse, and top management is unaware of them.

Seventy-two million people in the United States — seven of every ten workers — produce services, not goods. Measuring a service, whether you're in a barbershop or a warehouse, is much more difficult than counting the number of widgets a factory produces. A service may be difficult to measure but not impossible. A lot of warehouse managers and supervisors however, throw in the towel when it comes to measuring their employees' productivity. After the crews disperse among the racks, behind stacks, and inside trailers, supervisors seem to cross their fingers and hope that the workers are doing the right job, the right way, in the right amount of time. I think that warehouse companies cannot afford to operate that way any more. They should be particularly interested in measuring performance <u>because warehousing is a labor-intensive industry</u> and wages for 72 million people make up an enormous amount of money.

By measurement, I mean assigning a method and a time to a task. When I say "measurement," some people automatically think of industrial engineers and stopwatches. That's not always the case. The women working in the turkey processing plant didn't need a stopwatch. They set what they thought was a reasonable goal — 12,000 birds packaged in a shift — and measured their daily performance against it. Every warehouse, every distribution center, and

53

every company seems to have a different method for measuring productivity, many set by the improvisation of the employees.

I'll be the first to admit that there is a lot of opposition to performance standards. Many of you may dislike the thought of standards yourself. I think that unions, and some supervisors, resent and distrust measurement because they may have little influence on the decision-making process that goes into choosing a particular system. And forced change is threatening. The lack of information about measurement systems leaves too many valid questions unanswered. I'm convinced that there would be much less resistance to measurement if management would involve employees from all levels — middle management, supervisors, line workers.

To Measure or Not to Measure

I've found that without some sort of measurement system, productivity stagnates at 60 percent. On the other hand, implementing even a basic measuring system boosts productivity to 80 or 90 percent. Supervisors who cringe at the thought of installing a measurement system are missing the point; people want and need to know how they're doing. And if you don't provide a measuring system, the employees will come up with a system of their own like the workers in the turkey plant.

Whenever I think of measurement I am reminded of the game of golf. Would you play on a course if you didn't know the par for each hole, the distance to each tee and the general layout of the course? Probably not! In the same way, employees deserve to know exactly what kind of performance is expected of them. A measurement system defines and communicates those standards.

Without a measurement system, you waste time. Most of the problems that cause lower productivity are not the fault of the employee. Maybe you've realized this already, maybe you haven't. But if you have some sort of reporting system that tells you how much time tasks should require, and compare this against how much time it actually took, you can uncover problems that slow your employees down. These indirect costs and hidden lost time are the "gold nuggets" supervisors should grab first.

Using a reliable measurement system, you can learn a lot. Look for patterns, or trends, that might signal a problem. I remember one warehouse that had recently installed a reporting system. As I scanned through the reports, I noticed that a forklift driver, who usually performed at 85 percent, consistently dropped 60 percent one day a week. I asked his supervisor about those days, and he scratched his head.

"Hmmm, those are the days Pat doesn't work for me," he said. "Once a week, he's assigned to the back room. That's where operators have to pick individual items, like toothbrushes and aspirin from a sales order."

Pat, an ace forklift driver, wasn't trained to work in the backroom, and consequently took longer to fill the orders. Moreover, he wasn't comfortable working from a two-page list. There's a big difference between driving a forklift to pick full cases from a five to ten line order and individually hand-picking thirty items that go into a plastic tote. After we noticed the pattern and alerted the warehouse management to the problem, they trained someone else for the individual picking. The lack of measurement and feedback in this situation was costing the company many thousands of dollars.

Swimming In Hot Chocolate

A few years ago, I ran into a situation where a first line supervisor needed the right facts and figures to get support from management. One of the purchasing agents for a grocery warehouse found a great bargain on a shipment of cocoa mix. There was only one thing wrong. He bought it in February and it was received in the warehouse in May. Cocoa doesn't move very fast during the summer.

"We've got twenty-five pallets of cocoa out here, clogging up the shipping dock," Jay, a first line supervisor, told me. "We don't have enough space to store seasonal products. My crew is losing big chunks of time moving that cocoa mix from here to there, and back again."

The purchasing agent looked like a hero for finding a good deal on cocoa, but the supervisor's crew looked like they were performing below standard. I advised Jay to keep track of the amount of time his employees spent moving the mix around, so he could show management how much the "bargain" actually cost the company. His measurement system provided that information, which he brought to the warehouse manager.

You can see why it's important to keep records. With the right set of numbers, Jay could show management how much they paid to shift the cocoa mix around the warehouse. Next time the purchasing agent finds a bargain, he'll probably have to find another storage facility and pay for it from his budget.

The Means to an End

So far, I've focused on the reasons for using a measurement system, but there's something missing. How do you develop a practical system? It may be easier than you think. To take control of your work environment, you don't need to call in an industrial engineer with a stopwatch. What you need to do is attack the problems that consume the most money. In order to do that, you need to know which problems take the most time. There are essentially four methods a first line supervisor can use to develop measuring systems: estimating the time, history, work sampling, and engineered standards.

The first method uses judgement to predict the time needed for certain activities. Because these numbers are truly unscientific, their accuracy is only as good as the experience and background of the supervisor using them. The standards also depend on repetition and a certain amount of guesswork. If your crew loads pallets of oatmeal onto the same-sized truck every week, you probably have a pretty good idea how long the job takes. You can also use experience as a guide to estimate tasks you've never done before. For example, you may not have experience unloading snowblowers, but you discover that they are shipped in crates similar to those used for lawn mowers. Your crew has handled several shipments of mowers, and from that experience you can estimate the amount of time you'll need for the snowblowers. It's a good idea to keep a notebook in your pocket to record the time used for certain jobs.

If you use the history method, you'll run into one major drawback — time spent on problems is automatically built into your standard. That's what happened with the bicycle shipment I mentioned in the last chapter. In that case, the first line supervisor allowed two hours and forty-five minutes to unload the bicycles because that's how long it had always taken. That was their standard. Unfortunately, the standard was built around an inefficient method, and included a lot of lost time.

Work sampling is the third technique a first line supervisor can use to develop a measurement system. I think of this method as a modified form of auditing. The supervisor observes an employee, on a random basis, performing a task. This could be order selection, unloading, replenishment, break, talking to another worker, or time waiting to get around another worker. At the end of a period you total up the number of times each task has occurred. Divide into the total of all tasks, and you will have a percentage of the work day given to each task. You can now decide how much time should be spent on various tasks and compare this to the actual times to arrive at a productivity factor.

By accompanying the operator while he's working, you can clock the time used on the task, plus account for problems such as inefficient handling methods, late shipments, or mis-slotted products. When you measure by work sampling, it helps to divide the warehouse into sections with similar handling characteristics. Examples might include areas that are palletized, less-than-case or hand-pick lots, and large and small cases.

A work sampling audit provides the information you need to set up what I call scheduled expectancies (S/E's). First, the activity is scheduled, and second, it has an expectancy because you know it can be done in a certain amount of time. These scheduled expectancies must be reasonable when you set them up as norms to evaluate performance. For example, when we audited the unloading of the boxcar of bicycles, we set the S/E at one and a half hours. A one hour S/E would have been neither reasonable nor attainable. No group of workers could have done the job in so little time. On the other hand, the supervisor's previous estimate allowed nearly two and one half hours for unload-

61

ing the bicycles, — too much time. Of course, each warehouse and each group or function requires a different set of scheduled expectancies.

Of the four methods I've covered, engineered standards will probably give you the most accurate numbers. By definition, engineered standards reflect the time it takes a skilled employee to perform a task working at a pace that can be maintained for eight hours a day, without adverse physiological effects, and working under normal conditions. They may involve stopwatch time studies, or a predetermined standard time system that can be applied to a variety of activities, including stocking, sorting, ticketing and loading. Engineered standards are based on the best method for completing a task, as well as the time required. This is superior to the work sampling where standards are often based on methods and conditions that are not the best.

Although engineered standards offer the greater accuracy, they are not the only answer. Many managers feel that engineered standards are too much trouble to deal with so they do nothing. I have found that in most companies productivity information is available if you ask for it. There are a few steps a first line supervisor can take. You can keep track of productivity by getting two numbers. Productivity is best defined as units over hours, giving you a units per manhour figure. Some units of measure are: cases, pieces, line items, layers, and pallets. Both units and hours can be found in accounting, payroll or the computer department.

Set a goal or develop a historical number and compare this to what actually happened. Keep a daily record and to see trends, put the results on a graph.

Apples and Oranges

This chapter probably makes measurement systems sound simple to develop, and easy to implement. Unfortunately, they're neither simple nor easy. Chances are, the language of measurement is little more than mumbo-jumbo to the average warehouse worker. At the same time, employees (and supervisors, too) usually view new programs and the possibility of change with suspicious eyes. Often with good reason. Employees see new systems and standards as techniques for cutting payrolls, rather than as methods for improving productivity. I'm convinced that management at all levels — including the first line supervisor needs to be sensitive to the labor required where measurement is concerned. Sensitivity means creating accurate measurements that apply to specific tasks. It also calls for improved communication between management and employees, and greater involvement of warehouse workers in developing measurement standards.

Another way of being sensitive to labor involves comparing "apples to apples" when using standards. Let's say your unit of measurement is cases handled in a day. I hope they're all the same size, otherwise you're comparing one set of cases that measure six cubic feet with another set that

is one and a half cubic feet. Even if the case sizes match, one order may take 30 stops to pick 150 cases while another needs only three stops to get the same number. Measuring performance per piece requires some careful thought as well. Picking lawn mower hoods is a significantly different operation from pulling washers out of a bin and putting them in a bag.

Managing the Transition to Measurement

Whether or not your transition to standards goes smoothly depends a great deal on the way you present the program to employees. Measurement systems have a lot to offer employees, if they are used correctly. Standards help improve working conditions and customer service; they make work less frustrating and add greater consistency to the work cycle; they increase job security and improve the employee's sense of accomplishment.

One warehouse and trucking company did a good job of involving people in the development of a measurement system by introducing the new process to small groups of employees. The Vice President of Distribution told me later that there was very little resistance because the managers presented their program as a job security measure, not as a threat to "cut waste." He advised other firms to set up a measurement system not as a last-ditch effort to cut losses, but as a first step toward greater profitability and stability. In the long run, that means greater job security for every employee.

CHAPTER 5

TRAINING

Training

Kevin Fletcher was a broad-shouldered, 6'3" order selector, the kind of man who looks like he could take on a heavyweight boxer or replace a defensive tackle. He worked hard, too. While some of the other workers at Moser's Market warehouse lingered at the order desk, or over a cup of coffee at break, Kevin would be back at work, sweating his tail off in the aisles.

Everyone knew that Kevin was a steady performer. That's why his supervisor was surprised when the company's first performance report came out and Kevin Fletcher averaged only 70 percent. Compared to the effort he put into his work, it seemed odd that Kevin's performance was so low. After seeing a copy, the first line supervisor made a beeline for me, report in hand. I had been working with Moser's Market that summer, developing the system that generated Kevin's, and everyone else's, performance report.

"This one can't be accurate," he said, pointing at the number beside Kevin Fletcher's name. "Fletch is one of my hardest workers." After talking with the supervisor, I went over to introduce myself to Kevin, who looked frustrated by the whole affair.

"I don't understand why my percentage is so low," he said, shaking his head. "I mean, it's not as if I am a rookie. I've been with Moser's for almost three years. I'm doing my job the way I've always done it."

He'd Rather Walk Than Switch

Later that afternoon, I watched Kevin Fletcher pick an order. Everyone had been right; he did work hard. Kevin was sweating like a glass of beer on a hot day, obviously putting a lot of effort into every task. Then I realized why his performance rating was only so-so. Kevin was working hard, but he wasn't working smart. This is what I saw. When Fletcher entered an aisle he parked his pallet jack in the middle of the aisle, instead of parking it as close as possible to the racks. He took two extra steps to the slot to get a case and then walked two extra steps back to the jack with his hands full. After the shift finished for the day, I told Kevin and his supervisor that part of the mystery behind the low performance record was solved. I described the way Kevin was losing time walking between the pallet jack and the racks.

"I have a hard time believing that a few extra steps make much of a difference in my overall performance," Kevin Fletcher said. "As a matter of fact, it's probably saving me time." The supervisor nodded in agreement.

"An order selector who picks 150 pieces an hour, and walks four extra steps for each of those, adds up distance over an eight-hour shift. Those extra steps equal about 12,000 feet, over two miles."

To prove my point, I brought Kevin and his supervisor outside the warehouse and paced out a half-mile in the parking lot. "OK," I told Fletcher. "Walk over to that yellow sedan, and back again."

He did this without any trouble, but when he returned, I was waiting for him with a case of peas. Half of the time Kevin spent walking in the aisles, he carried a load. He just looked at me and said, "Forget it, I see what you mean."

Walking a mile takes about 20 minutes, even if you travel at a steady clip. You may be ox-strong, but carrying a load will slow you down and tire you out faster than following a more efficient method. And that lowers your performance record. Kevin Fletcher is a case in point. When he stopped hoofing the aisles and started using the pallet jack in the way it was intended (parking next to the racks instead of in the middle of the aisle), Kevin's performance improved and he discovered that he wasn't as tired at the day's end. Moser's Market came out ahead, too, because Kevin had more time for productive work.

Moral of the Story

Kevin Fletcher's experience shows that **training an employee to use the right methods can make a big physical — and fiscal — difference.** A few years back, the University of Michigan conducted a study in which 50 percent of the workers polled said they didn't have enough information to perform their jobs properly. Fifty percent! I look at that figure and see a lot of wasted job satisfaction — and wasted money.

Where do employees get the information they need to do their jobs? I believe it's in training. And the buck stops with first line supervisors, because they are the ones who are responsible for the training of their employees. When a supervisor points a blaming finger at an employee for shoddy work habits, he's forgetting who is responsible for that employee's performance. Who's at fault if an order picker walks instead of using the pallet jack? The pointing finger aims straight between the supervisor's eyes. I call it the boomerang effect. **The supervisor is the one responsible for giving employees the information they need to do their jobs right.**

A Construction Job for Supervisors

Training is not only a responsibility, it's an opportunity to shape the work environment. If you allow your employees to be trained on the job by someone else (or not at all), you forfeit your big chance to affect the performance of your work crew. In the last few chapters, I have focused on the tools a first line supervisor needs to create a positive work environment. It's like building a house, step-by-step. The foundation of the supervisor's building is job definition — understanding his responsibility, accountability and authority. After laying the foundation, the first line supervisor can begin placing the building blocks: time management to organize and set priorities, and measurement to track progress toward goals.

**The corner stone of a positive work environment is
training, because it affects every other aspect of warehouse work.** If the corner stone is laid crooked, the whole
building will be askew. In the same way, employees who
don't have the right information may cause errors and
delays. If a supervisor trains his employees well, however,
they can do the work right the first time. In the long run,
that will save time, money and frustration for everyone.

The purpose of training is to simplify work, to get rid of
unnecessary motions such as the extra steps from the pallet
jack to the pallet of cases. **Training picks up where
measurement leaves off. Measurement assigns a
method to a task, and training teaches employees to use
that method.** A supervisor needs both training and measurement, because the two are like a hammer and nail, not
much good without each other. While measurement is the
nail that connects the different steps of a task, training is
the hammer that reinforces those methods.

Methods Without Madness

If there's one thing I know about work methods, it is this:
they have to be consistent. Without adequate training and
an emphasis on the most effective methods, each employee
will develop his own way of doing things. Not too long
ago I was watching several workers loading pallets into the
truck. The cases were different sizes, so the workers on the
dock wrapped strapping tape around them to prevent

shifting in the truck. That was fine, until I looked closer. Each employee used a different amount of tape. As few as four, and as many as twelve rounds of tape held the cases together. I don't need to tell you that it takes twice as long to wrap eight rounds as it does four.

Which way was right? None of them and all of them, because management had not defined the proper method. When customer service announced that "We want the product to arrive at the customer on the pallet, not all over the truck," someone in distribution decided that the best way to accomplish that would be to wrap tape around the cases. Unfortunately, the decision-making process ended there, without anyone asking "How much tape?" As a result, each operator defined the method for himself.

I believe that the company and the supervisor, not individual operators, should choose the methods to be used. Although using different amounts of strapping tape may seem petty, it shows how common inconsistent methods can be. I bet you could go out on the warehouse floor tomorrow and find two employees doing the same job using different methods. The problem is an expensive one. The extra tape cost money, and so did the extra time spent wrapping the cases more securely than was necessary.

Why the Supervisor?

When the supervisor trains his employees, it is not a mission of mercy. **You, the supervisor, stand to gain at**

least as much from consistent training as the company and the employee. For one thing, it will force you to learn the methods so that you can teach them to others. We've all had bosses from the "Do as I say, not as I do" school of management. That system doesn't win friends or influence people. Workers are more willing to respect supervisors who know the job themselves. Gaining employee respect will build confidence and make you feel more comfortable in your role as first line supervisor. That's especially welcome if you're new on the job.

The first line supervisor's job depends on his employees — another good reason why you should train them. Think of your performance review. How are you judged? What is your output? Under most systems, your performance is based on the quality of your employees' performance. If my reputation depended on a bunch of other people, I would want to make darn sure that they were doing things right. And the best way to do that is by training them myself.

I've found that **training also improves communication between the first line supervisor and his employees.** Think about it! You are the one who walks through the task with the worker, showing him the correct method. Later, if that same employee stumbles across a problem, who will hear about it? My bet is that you will. Training provides the perfect opportunity for a supervisor to lay out clear expectations for an employee. It sets up an open line of communication between the two, so that the operator

feels comfortable asking the supervisor questions or suggesting possible improvements.

Playing Telephone Tag

Without the link of training, communication between the first line supervisor and his employees can be like the old game of telephone. You remember that one: a "secret" is passed from ear to ear around a circle of people until the person at the end of the line compares the now-garbled message with the original.

An engineer once told me a story about his experience in a grocery warehouse where he was doing some auditing. He noticed that the selectors had a curious way of filling orders. Although most orders called for coffee, the selectors passed the coffee slot to pick every other item on the order. Then they doubled back to put the java on top of the pallet. It wasn't just one or two workers. All of them filled orders this way. When the engineer asked them why they doubled back, the order selectors said "We were told to do it that way."

The engineer reported this to the first line supervisor. "That's not right," he said. "I told them the coffee should be visible so the customers can count it, not that it had to go on top."

Coffee is one of the most expensive dry grocery items a retail store can stock. So whenever customers discovered that their coffee order was short, the warehouse management heard about it — and so did the first line supervisor. The supervisor's solution was to stack the coffee so that customers could count it easily. Unfortunately, he never wrote down the method or showed the employees exactly what he meant. By the time the instructions filtered down to the order selectors, they heard that management wanted all coffee to go on top of the pallet, even if it meant doubling back at the end of an order. This example is just like a game of telephone, except this mix-up cost the company real money.

No Time Like the Present

If you believe that training employees is part of your job, and that it benefits everybody in the company, let's get started. And the best place to do that is in the hiring process. I think it's pointless to accept responsibility for the performance of your employees if you don't see them until they start work for you. Go to management and lobby for more influence in the hiring decisions that affect you.

Until you gain some influence, you'll have to start training on Day One. Think about the last time you had a "new kid on the block." The work load probably didn't stand still while you introduced the new recruit around the floor, and you might not have had the time to chat about career goals. No, usually a rookie gets "thrown to the lions" on his first day, or assigned to a veteran who is supposed to show him the ropes.

Although your day is busy enough already, starting a new employee off on the right foot is important enough to do it right. The orientation doesn't have to take all day. Set aside an hour or so to meet with the recruit to introduce yourself and the company. This could take place on the first day, or a few days before he starts his first shift. If your company uses an employee manual, review that with the new employee, pointing out the key procedures. Later, if you do pair the rookie with a veteran worker, check up on him frequently so that the new employee knows that he is responsible to <u>you</u>. Take the time to give him an overview of the major clients and products he'll be dealing with in his job. Paint the big picture so that the new employee can see where he fits in. An orientation like this is a small initial investment that will yield big returns in employee loyalty and motivation.

One of the modern tools available today is the video camera. Most companies have both the camera and the playback equipment. Video-tape jobs that are being done in a proper manner. This tape is now a valuable tool that can be used both for newcomer training and for periodic reviews with everyone doing those jobs.

New employees aren't the only ones that need training. When procedures change (as new machines or products arrive), the methods used to handle them must change, too. It's important for the first line supervisor to define the new method and teach it to the employees. I'm not talking about classroom teaching. There's no need for that at all. **Training should be as practical and hands-on as pos-**

sible. And it's not enough to just tell people what to do. You have to tell them how to do it. The "how" training really tells the story, because the extra steps a worker uses to complete a task consume both time and energy.

For example, it's not enough to tell your employees to "Put a label on each of those cases." I've seen five men do it three different ways. Spell it out for them. "The method I want you to use is to pull the label off it's backing while you're entering the slot, and put it on the case with a sweeping motion of your hand." It might help to explain why there is a specific method for a task that seems so trivial. A warehouse worker can handle more than 3,000,000 cases a year. If he spends one half second extra putting a label on each case, those accumulated seconds total 40 hours, or one wasted work week a year.

Let me introduce you to the type of worker I call the Bricklayer. You may have worked with this fastidious employee. He'll put cases on the pallet and then adjust them by patting them on this side and straightening them on that side, so that they're all lined up — just like a mason smoothing mortar around bricks. By the time he's done, he's probably handled that pallet of cases four times. While it's nice that the Bricklayer cares about the quality of his work, his extra effort is not necessarily worthwhile. Does the company want to pay for those extra motions when the cases will all shift during loading and shipping anyway? Probably not. The matter seems trivial until you stop to consider that the Bricklayer may also spend a half second more than necessary on each case, which adds up to 40 hours lost time a year. There is too much waste in most distribution companies!

Step By Step

When you know the "how" methods of a task, it's easier to explain them to others. Talk through the job first, showing how each step relates to the others. If you are training your crew to label cases, explain that the method calls for simul-taneous, rather than separate, motions: pulling the label off the backing while entering the slot, grabbing the case with one hand, placing the label on the case with the other hand. Allow the employee to practice a few times while you watch. Emphasize the correct methods rather than speed, which will come later.

Training is a continuous process, not a one-time event. The first line supervisor should work with new people at least two or three times to bring them up to speed and observe their methods. Follow up on the training sessions by periodically evaluating all employees. This is important because all workers develop their own work habits over time, including some that aren't compatible with the correct methods.

During the training process, ask for feedback and sugges-tions from the people on your crew. This can be the most helpful information of all. Employees are usually the

experts when it comes to their jobs. Let them teach you so you can be a better teacher, too. Although I think the supervisor should define the best methods, allowing an employee to contribute helps that person feel a sense of ownership in his job, and lets him know that he's a part of the whole operation.

A Blueprint for Success

When carpenters build a house, they work from a blueprint, a valuable sheet that gives them the big picture (the floor plan), along with the details (like the position of electrical outlets). Training is the supervisor's blueprint; he uses training to tell his employees how they fit into the company, as well as teaching them the best method for labeling cases.

A good plan and sound construction will result in a well-built building. Similarly, a continuous, practical training program will help create a goal-oriented atmosphere that encourages questions, consistent methods, and good performance. Like a carpenter, the first line supervisor has the ability to build something from scratch. Training is one more tool to help the supervisor create a positive work environment.

CHAPTER 6

BARRIERS TO PRODUCTIVITY

Barriers To Productivity

It was raining hard as I threaded my way through the warehouse to the loading dock. Just as I rounded the corner by the shipping docks, a thunderclap boomed overhead. Weather like this made me glad I was inside looking out. This was several years ago, while I toured the operation of one of our clients, a large grocery chain.

I could hear the rain lashing against the trucks as they backed up to the loading dock. Luckily, the dock canopies covering the shipping doors were in place and kept the wind and water outside. As usual the arriving trucks were slightly higher than the loading dock, so that the dockplates slanted from the truck beds to the cement floor. Everything seemed to be going fine until I noticed water on the dockplate. A quick look overhead told me that one canopy had pulled loose from the wall letting the rain fall on the dock plate.

Raindrops Kept Falling on His Head

Bruce, one of the forklift drivers, tried several times to drive up the slippery dockplate, but with little luck. After each attempt, he backed up to try again. The forklift shot forward, but could only spin its wheels on the wet ramp. I felt like I was watching a boxing match, and the rain-soaked ramp was winning.

Finally, I couldn't take it anymore. Before Bruce could

turn the forklift around, I tapped him on the shoulder. "How long has the canopy been loose like that?" I asked.

Bruce stopped to think. "About six or seven months, I'd say."

"It doesn't look very safe," I said, "especially with the dockplate at such an angle. Has anyone ever slipped off?"

"Yeah," Bruce said. "Randy fell off about three weeks ago. Bruised his shoulder."

All those months, and nobody had repaired the doorlock. This is how I imagined the situation: the employees paid attention to the gaping doorlock only when it rained, and then nobody wanted to get wet trying to fix it. When it was sunny, of course, the workers had no problem. But the loose canopy created problems for everyone involved. The wet dockplate not only wasted time, it was dangerous. The first line supervisor should have had the damage repaired before anyone was hurt and if not then, surely after the accident occurred.

Roadblocks to Great Performances

This incident typifies what I call a barrier to productivity. **Barriers are situations that require extra time and effort, problems that set up roadblocks to 100 percent performance.** Sometimes the roadblocks as obvious as a barricade with flashing red lights. Obvious roadblocks in the warehouse, like blocked lanes or absenteeism, immediately show that your crew is losing time. The loose door-lock and the water on the dockplate should have warned the supervisor that a problem was preventing the loading crew from doing its best. Roadblocks are often inconspicuous. These hidden barriers are just as serious as the obvious ones. Think of the unexpected potholes and railroad crossings that delay the unprepared driver, or the broken pallets, machinery breakdowns, and shorts that detour warehouse time.

As a first line supervisor, you are responsible for your employees' performance. That's why it is your job to dismantle the roadblocks that lower their productivity — whether the problems are obvious or not. **The first step in removing a productivity barrier is to identify its source.** Only then can you get at the heart of the problem. My experience tells me that roadblocks to productivity generally fall into one of five categories:

- Employees don't know what is expected of them.

- They don't know how to do the job.

- They can't perform the job as it is defined.

- They run into organizational barriers.

- They don't want to do the job.

Like Ripples in a Pond

The first two reasons are closely tied to communication and training. **As a supervisor, you have to clearly define and explain the expectations you place on your employees.** If an order selector does not know what you consider a job well done, it's unlikely he'll meet your expectations.

Poor training is the main reason employees lack the know-how to perform their work. I'm willing to bet that poor training accounts for the majority of lost time in most warehouses. Why? Because the problems that stem from inadequate training do not stay in one place. Their effect spreads to other areas of the warehouse, like ripples from a rock thrown into a pond.

For example, the productivity of one distribution warehouse suffered because its shipping docks were always congested. The traffic jams delayed shipments and turned a few hairs gray for the first line supervisor. Relieving the traffic flow proved difficult until the supervisor identified the source of the problem. The docks were not jammed because there were too many orders, or too few employees. They were congested because the loaders had not been trained properly.

As often happens, the different-sized cases made the loads unstable on the pallets, so this particular crew used an automatic stretch-wrapping machine to stabilize pallets for shipping. But instead of using the correct method — wrapping one pallet and loading the finished one at the same time — the employees stood and watched as the machine wrapped plastic around and around the cases. While they waited for the stretch-wrapper to finish its job, orders piled up on the dock. These delays seemed minor to the workers, but like a pebble in a pond, they sent out ripples that affected the rest of the shipping operation. When the employees started using the correct wrapping method, the dock congestion disappeared.

Improper training not only makes employees work harder while producing fewer results, it also hurts their motivation. I've heard it said: "If they don't care enough to tell me to do the job, then they obviously don't care how it's done." Wipe your slate clean of this barrier and put your limited time and energy where it really counts, up front with an effective, consistent training program.

Rooting for the Good Guys

The third type of productivity barrier — when the employee cannot perform the work — usually involves a physical limitation. An example might be a person who is too weak to lift cases or doesn't have enough dexterity to operate the equipment. It's up to management, including the first line supervisor, to decide how to handle these situations; whether to make exceptions in performance standards for these employees or to raise hiring requirements.

When Pallet Jacks Feel Run-Down

The fourth roadblock to productivity — organizational barriers — are often the most frustrating, and the most unnecessary. These problems are caused by procedures, equipment, or bureaucracy — snafu's that are beyond the control of the employees. Sometimes they're minor irritants that take a little extra time, like a broken pallet or an out-of-the-way order desk. At their worst, however, organizational barriers operate like a form of water torture, wearing away the productivity and spirit of your work crew. These barriers are the empty slots or missing products that send order selectors on a wild goose chase; the delays caused by computer mix-ups; the equipment that falls apart for lack of maintenance.

I once helped a warehouse company set up a reporting system to track the time spent on various tasks. After reviewing the first batch of reports, a supervisor noticed that the order selectors lost time each shift because of equipment problems. It turned out that the batteries on the double pallet jacks lost power during the eight hour shift. Every time a battery started to run down an employee had to go to the battery charging area, across the warehouse to get a freshly charged battery. The company lost $2,000 a week because of these battery changes. That's a hefty organizational barrier. Once the problem was identified, however, the supervisor suggested solutions. He recommended purchasing a better battery that ran 14 to 16 hours

without charging, and he ordered a fresh battery installed at the start of each shift.

Many of you know the helpless, frustrated feeling that comes with a flooded basement. The rain trickles in as fast as you mop it up. That's the same feeling warehouse workers (including first line supervisors) get when they run into organizational barriers day after day. The feelings may be similar, but the approach to solving the problem is completely different. When their basement continually floods, most people install a sump pump or water-proofing. But that's not the approach taken in the warehouse industry. Employees often complain about problems, while maintaining an attitude that seems to say "That's just the way it is. There is nothing we can do about it."

That's not true. I want to tell you that you don't have to accept barriers to productivity as standard operating procedures. These problems are not a natural part of warehouse life, and neither are the frustrations, negative attitudes, and low productivity that accompany them. By removing these organizational stumbling blocks and all the other road-blocks to productivity, you can make the warehouse a better place to work.

A final type of productivity barrier occurs when employees don't want to work. This is a motivational problem. There are bound to be some troublemakers on every crew — that's human nature. But I believe that most people want to do a good job. **Given the correct tools and information,**

the majority of employees will perform as well as they can. Time and time again I've seen first line supervisors focus their energy on the troublemakers in their crews. Supervisors are responsible for the productivity of all their employees, yet they get all wrapped up in fighting these rebels. The supervisors seem to think that "If only I could get rid of them, my problems would be solved." I hate to break the news to you, but when those troublemakers go, the company will probably hire a couple more just like them.

Supervisors who become obsessed with the troublemakers in their work crews might take a lesson from a manager I met several years ago. We installed a reporting system with performance standards in a large distribution warehouse that was averaging 75 percent productivity. Rich, the manager, told me "I'm going to use that information to get rid of the employees who aren't performing."

I shook my head. "Rich, I think you've got your priorities wrong. You have 200 people working for you around the clock. How many do you figure are troublemakers?"

"I suppose it's three or four percent." he said.

"Okay," I said. "At the most, that's 8 employees. Even if you doubled their output, it wouldn't add much to your total productivity. You need to spend your energy on the majority of your employees - the other 96 percent."

Two years later, I saw Rick at a meeting and asked him how things were going. "You know," he said, "I didn't believe you at first. But I took your advice, and it really does work to focus on managing the majority of the crew. I still have some troublemakers. But we're up to 92 percent performance now, and because of that I have 170 people in the warehouse, instead of 200. It's a lot easier for me to manage now."

Only a small percentage of your employees perform their job poorly on purpose. So why waste your time on them? You'll have more success helping those who want to do better. Rewards and encouragement, not punishment, create a positive work environment.

From Stumbling Blocks to Stepping Stones

Imagine if only 6 out of every 10 employees showed up for work. Or if every employee performed his job with one hand tied behind his back. Most management teams would not allow such substandard performance, right? Wrong. **The warehouse that does not have goals or standards and a good feedback system has a standard productivity rate of 60 percent of their potential.** You may not see the ropes that bind your employees' hands, but they are there.

The volume of products passing through warehouses is so great that every minute lost or gained can account for thousands of dollars a year. That's why improving productivity is so important. For example, if a warehouse worker handles 150 cases an hour, or 300,000 cases a year and you can shave off one penny a case by using a better method or solving a problem, you'll save $3,000 per employee. If you oversee a crew of 10, that will total $30,000 — enough for a first line supervisor's salary.

I'm willing to bet that you can raise the productivity level in your area from the standard 60 percent to 80 percent or more, without major layout changes, without buying new equipment, and without installing fancy systems. If the productivity of your company does not concern you, it should. For one thing, **getting rid of the barriers that delay your employees is a basic part of your job.** Another reason is that higher productivity helps the company remain profitable, and that means job security for you. Improving your employees' performance will help them feel good about their work, and make your job more rewarding as well.

The individual supervisor can make a big difference, but improving productivity will require some effort on your part. It takes a special skill to recognize the barriers that consume your crew's time and energy. When you rush through each day, dealing with issues that need your attention now, it's tough to notice a slow pallet jack or the cause of the congested loading dock. But it can be done! Try to take a fresh look at the operations you see every day, and ask yourself: Is there a better way to do this? What are the most effective methods? How can we improve our

performance?

With a keen eye, some fancy footwork, and an open ear you can actively prevent or solve problems that disrupt the flow of work. For some first line supervisors, it may be as simple as spending more time walking around the warehouse floor. Other supervisors may need to provide better training and feedback on their employees' performance. However you do it, identify and remove the productivity barriers that are within your control. Together you can take these stumbling blocks and change them into stepping stones that lead to a better working environment for everyone.

CHAPTER 7

COMMUNICATION: A TWO-WAY STREET

Communication: A Two-Way Street

Frank Sovitz sat near the conference room door, chair tilted on its back legs, his arms folded across his barrel chest. He looked ready to bolt for the door. A glance at his watch told Frank that the training session was almost over, and he was glad. The distribution company where Frank supervised the second shift had hired the consultant to improve the group's communication skills. "Get to know your employees," the speaker told the class of physical distribution managers and supervisors. "The workers are the ones who make the operation hum. Spend more time talking with them out on the floor." The message went in one ear and out the other, as far as Frank Sovitz was concerned. He'd heard it all before. At the close of the session, the speaker gave the class an assignment for the following week: to talk with every one of their employees before the next session, even if only to say, "Hello." Most of the managers shrugged their shoulders and nodded, as if to say, "This won't be tough."

That was Frank Sovitz's reaction, too. He was convinced that his communication skills needed little improvement. "I don't need this 'touchy-feely' stuff," Frank thought. "I talk to my people all the time."

Clean Sweep

The next day, Frank arrived at work at his usual time. As

he walked through the warehouse on his way to the office, Frank noticed Carl, the janitor, sweeping near the door.

"Morning, Carl" Frank said as he passed the long-time employee. Carl looked up to return the greeting, but when he saw who it was, he dropped his broom in surprise. Frank, who had reached his office door by this time, turned at the sound of the broom hitting the floor. There stood Carl, eyes wide.

The scene opened Frank Sovitz's eyes, too. "Now that I think about it, I can't remember the last time I talked with Carl," Frank admitted to himself. "I guess my communication skills aren't as good as I thought."

Profiting From His Mistakes

Frank Sovitz soon learned a lesson from his chance meeting with Carl the janitor: It pays to communicate with employees. The two men crossed paths in the hall one afternoon and Carl cleared his throat.

"I think you ought to know we're wasting money on some of our supplies," Carl said. "The way it is now, we buy cleaning solvents pre-mixed, which costs more and takes up a lot of storage space. It might be cheaper to get the dry stuff and mix it ourselves."

Frank reexamined the supply orders and learned that the premixed cleaners did indeed cost more. At Carl's suggestion, new supplies were ordered in powder form. The company saved $100 a month as a result. And all it cost Frank Sovitz was a simple morning greeting. Those words bridged the communication gap so that Carl felt comfortable approaching Frank with his cost-cutting idea.

The Talking Tool

Frank Sovitz was lucky. He quickly learned the dollar and cents value of communication. Sure, he saved the company some money, but he also gained a valuable ally in Carl. You can make good use of this lesson, too. Communication is another tool that the first line supervisor can use to create a positive work environment. Learning how to communicate more effectively is not an optional skill. Imagine what running a warehouse would be like without forklifts or pallet jacks. Every task would be tougher and take longer. That's what ineffective communication does to an operation — it makes everyone's job more difficult. Machines are necessary for your operation, and so is communication.

You may be a mechanical genius or an organizational wizard, but you can't succeed as an effective supervisor unless you know how to talk with, and listen to, your employees, That is why this chapter deals with some communication skills that you can put into practice today.

Upward and Onward

Communication flows in two directions within organizations: downward and upward. Downward communication refers to the steady stream of reports, forms, memos and meetings flowing from management to employees. Downward communication is necessary and useful, but only if it's balanced by upward communication, from employees to management. Through upward communication, workers tell their supervisor about actual or potential problems, as well as opportunities for cost savings and increased output. You can create a work environment that encourages this kind of communication.

What's in it for you? For one thing, the workers out on the warehouse floor are your eyes and ears; they can often spot problems long before you notice them. For another, communication involves employees in the operation, letting them play a more active role in their work. And **communication ultimately improves productivity.** A majority of the employees surveyed in a 1980 U.S. Chamber of Commerce study said they performed better when sharing and using information about their work, instead of passively receiving instructions. People want to work and succeed, but you must help them by creating an environment that fosters effective communication. In the long run, it'll make your job more rewarding, too.

Priming the Pump

Encouraging your employees to send more information up the line is like priming a water pump. At first, you'll have to put some water into the pipes by digging for news and

asking questions. After the pressure builds, however, you'll see the results of your efforts in a steady flow of information from your crew. Here are some steps you can take to accomplish this:

- Keep employees informed.

- Be visible.

- Be receptive.

- Take action.

Downward communication primes the pump for upward communication; that's why you should keep your employees informed. **Workers from every level need to understand what's going on with the company.** And you should be the one to tell your employees how their performance fits into the company as a whole.

Too often, workers rely on the grapevine for information that should come from their supervisor or manager. Don't let this happen. The rumor mill breeds uncertainty, misinformation, and resentment. Direct information from management, however, inspires trust and builds rapport with employees. Pass along positive or negative comments regarding your crew's performance, whether these remarks come from managers or customers. Similarly, update them on the company's status. If the warehouse is losing money, tell the people who can do something about it — the employees. When things are going well, let them know so they can be proud of a job well done.

Describe your objectives, as well as management's long-term goals, to your employees. This links them to the operation with a greater sense of responsibility and owner-ship. Also, when they know your objectives, employees can focus on specific areas to determine what information is most valuable to pass along. For example, if improving warehouse security is your top priority this month, your crew can keep their eyes open for potential problems in that area and suggest improvements. They'll know what to look for, and you won't be sifting through a ton of well-meaning comments about topics other than security.

Take a Walk

You can also invite upward communication by increasing your visibility. This tactic is often called "management by walking around," and involves spending more time out on the floor, talking with individual employees. **Walking around generates communication, as well as motivation.** If employees see you out on the loading dock, or in the hall, they may feel more comfortable volunteering information. An office with a big desk can be an intimidating place.

Employees respect those managers and supervisors who know their people and their operation. Wouldn't you? I'll never forget the time one physical distribution manager took me on a tour of his warehouse. As we walked around the second floor, he bragged about his efficient system for unloading the elevators, often a bottleneck in multi-story warehouses. When we got to the first elevator, there was no sign of the system the manager had mentioned, so he asked one of the operators, "Where's the automatic unloader?"

"We haven't used that system in a couple of years," the employee replied.

Although I felt sorry for the manager, he was clearly oblivious to the everyday operation of his warehouse. You can prevent this from happening to you by getting out on the floor several times a day to ask questions, encouraging suggestions and respond to comments. Set a goal of visiting with each employee at least once a week. You'll learn more about the operation, while getting to know the people who make the warehouse run.

Reaping What You Sow

I'm not saying that you'll be bombarded with suggestions and goodwill every time you venture out on the floor. Developing rapport with your employees takes a little cultivation before you can reap the benefits.

I learned this lesson in one of my early jobs as an industrial engineer assigned to perform time studies in a punch press department. As you know, industrial engineers and stopwatches are about as popular as pink eye in a daycare center. The veteran workers were a surly bunch, and their main source of entertainment seemed to be heckling the latest engineer. A succession of time-study people had passed through the department before my turn came.

Those machine operators never loved me, but they did eventually accept me. By the time I left the department two years later, I knew those people better that their manager did. It was no magic. I did it by talking with them. I made the rounds every day, listening to the employees talk about their work, their families, their politics. Over several months, I gained their trust.

There's another way to manage by walking around. One manager I know keeps a 3- by 5-inch index card for each employee. Listed on the card are the employee's name, age, and birthday, plus information about wedding anniversaries, hobbies, or family members' names. The manager uses this card system to personalize his dealings with employees (by sending birthday cards, for example). Without costing a lot in time or money, the system is effective because it communicates a personal interest in your employees.

Management by walking around creates a positive work environment by showing employees that you care as much about them as you do about their performance. In an environment like this, employees are more likely to work with supervisors and managers to share information, spot problems, and find solutions. But in order to take the

first step toward that kind of teamwork, you have to "take a walk."

All Ears

The next step in encouraging upward communication is to be receptive. Communicating with employees should be a conversation with plenty of give and take. That means you have to stop talking long enough to hear what your employees have to say. Sometimes, however, conversations turn into lectures, and people talk your ears off without leaving you room to reply. Management often treats employees this way by setting policies that directly affect their jobs, with little regard for employee input.

It shouldn't be this way. If the conversation between you and your employees is too one-sided, open your ears. **Communication is a two-way street: Everyone needs to listen, as well as talk.** Consider the tasks that fill your days — meetings, telephone calls, talking with employees and customers, reporting to your boss. As human resource managers, first line supervisors may spend the bulk of their day listening in one way or another.

Unfortunately, many of us aren't as good as we could be when it comes to listening. Consider the time you spend in school learning reading, writing and arithmetic. Now compare that with your coursework in listening. If you're like me, there's not much to compare. Little wonder there are communications gaps.

You can bridge these gaps by being receptive. Listen to your employees, admit your mistakes, and let them challenge your policies. Accept the bad news with the good, and if a report from the floor spells trouble, focus your anger or frustration on the problem itself. Don't rail at the messenger who brought the news. Also, when an employee stops in your office, treat his visit as a source of information, not as an interruption.

Act Now, Don't Hold Your Peace

Soliciting communication from employees is not enough. You must complete the communication cycle by acting on the information you've been given. I've often heard workers say, "What's the use in telling management? Nobody's going to do anything about it anyway." If you fail to take action, you'll encourage a cynical attitude. You'll also risk stifling a valuable source of information — your employees.

I remember reading about a manufacturing company that asked for employee feedback about management errors and other barriers to productivity. As a result of the program, the plant saw its productivity double in a few years. The suggestions themselves were only part of the reason for the productivity gains, however. Management tracked employee comments and made sure that action was taken on each one. This assured workers that their ideas went farther than somebody's circular file. Because management sincerely wanted employee feedback, and acted on

the information, employees willingly passed along their observations. **Actions are a form of communication, and they often speak louder than words.**

Like Sand Through an Hourglass

The flow of upward communication does not end with the first line supervisor. On the contrary, the process I've discussed in this chapter applies as well to the way the supervisor and his manager should communicate. How you handle this relationship will affect the communication climate for the rest of the operation.

The communication patterns in the warehouse are like the flow of sand in an hourglass. The sand accurately measures time by flowing slowly, but steadily, through the narrow waist of the hourglass. In the same way, communication moves between management and workers via the first line supervisor. Information travels back and forth simultaneously, however, as if the hourglass were constantly being turned over.

You can see why the role of the first line supervisor is an important one: he sifts through information coming from both directions, passes along the most valuable bits. The supervisor must stay on top of the job by keeping the lines of communication open. If not, the blocked lines create a bottleneck that adds pressure on all sides.

Ultimately, it's in your best interest to improve commu-

nication between employees and management. Encourage upward communication from your work crew: get out on the floor, listen to their problems and suggestions, and act on issues within your authority. Likewise, keep your manager informed of developments on the warehouse floor. As often as you can, talk with your boss informally; don't wait for the crisis session, monthly meeting, or yearly review.

Remember that effective communication skills are a necessary set of tools for the first line supervisor, not an optional one. Start using those tools today — you'll be glad you did, and so will your co-workers.

CHAPTER 8

MONTIVATION AND POSITIVE REINFORCEMENT

Motivation and Positive Reinforcement

The word was out: Micro Distribution Center (MDC), a small public warehouse, was finally converting from straight line to the Z-pick method. The Z-pick wasn't really a new method by most standards, but Al Boyd was still excited at the prospect of introducing his crew to the system. Al had been supervising MDC's second shift for three months, but he left work every night feeling he hadn't accomplished much. Managing the transition to the new method would prove his leadership skills, Al thought. This might be his big chance to show management that they had made the right choice in making him a first line supervisor.

In the days following the order, Al read everything he could find about the Z-pick. The young supervisor learned that the method was tailor-made for companies like MDC that picked mainly individual cases. Armed with all the information available, Al proceeded to train his crew in the Z-pick. He told them that the method allows order selectors to build a better, more efficient, pallet load. Next, he showed them how to load cases from alternating sides of an aisle without backtracking or walking around the pallet jack. Then Al sat back and waited for the performance reports to show how much the Z-pick had improved his crew's productivity.

He waited ... and waited. Over the course of the next few weeks, Al Boyd reached an uncomfortable conclusion. Instead of a steady climb, the crew's performance level was taking a nose-dive. Not only were his employees ignoring the new method, but they were doing worse than before. While the reporting system showed that the crew's productivity was slipping, a quick walk around the warehouse told Al that the crew's morale was sinking, too. Some of the most dependable employees started coming to work late. The percentage of damaged cases per load doubled in three weeks. And formerly friendly operators turned a cold shoulder when they saw Al coming.

They Want a Piece of the Action

The first line supervisor couldn't figure it out. The workers knew the correct Z-pick methods, but weren't using them, even though the new system would make their jobs easier. Frustrated by what he called the crew's bad attitude, Al talked it over with Jerry, a loader and longtime friend.
"Why are the order selectors being so bull-headed?" Al asked Jerry. "The Z-pick isn't that tough. Why can't they follow the method they learned in training?"
Jerry shook his head. "It's not that simple. The crew never understood why we had to change methods in the first place. The old way seemed to work just fine."
"But 'just fine' wasn't good enough." Al said. "The Z-pick takes less time and less energy. It'll benefit the workers at least as much as the company."
"If you had explained it that way, the pickers might have cooperated." Jerry said. "I suppose we just want a say in decisions that affect our job. Nobody likes to have new things jammed down their throats."

How Does Your Garden Grow?

Al Boyd had good intentions when he introduced his crew
to the Z-pick. Unfortunately, good intentions weren't
enough to convince the employees to accept the new
system. First, there was a communication gap. Al Boyd
knew the reasons for Micro Distribution Center's switch to
the Z-pick, but he didn't pass that information on to his
crew. The employees didn't understand the need for a new
method, and considered Al's silence a sign that management didn't care what they thought.

Al Boyd's second mistake was thinking that once he
trained his order selectors in the new method, it was only a
matter of time until their productivity improved. He
learned the hard way that **the attitude of employees affects
job performance as much as their ability.** Although Al's
employees had learned the Z-pick, they didn't have the
desire to use it. Instead of waiting for them to accept the
new method, Al should have been out on the floor with
encouragement and support. You can plant the most
expensive seeds in your garden, but if you don't water and
weed them, they probably won't take root. In the same
way, it's little wonder that the Z-pick didn't prosper with
Al's crew.

Great Performances

**It is your role as first line supervisor to nurture employ-
ees, to help them perform to the best of their ability.**

118

But first you must be able to define "good performance." You are the middleman when it comes to setting goals and expectations for employees. First, you need to verify management's priorities to learn how your employees should focus their energies. Then, you must interpret management's expectations by setting specific goals, telling your employees what kind of performance you expect. When employees understand a task's purpose, they become more motivated to perform well.

Improving and maintaining job performance is the heart of the first line supervisor's role. You already have many of the tools necessary to create a work environment that encourages productivity: job definition, time management, training, measurement, communication. Two final tools I'm adding to that list are motivation and positive reinforcement. These skills work together to encourage and maintain job performance.

People Who Need People

Motivation is the fuel that drives people to accomplish things. When you motivate someone, you're kindling that fuel, inspiring in them the will or desire to get things done. Several years ago, psychologist Abraham Maslow said that satisfying people's needs will motivate them. He illustrated this theory with a pyramid, which showed the levels of needs from bottom to top: physiological, security, social, self-esteem, and self-fulfillment. Each need level, according to Maslow, must be satisfied before the one

119

above it can be addressed.

As a first line supervisor, you have little or no control over the first two levels on Maslow's pyramid: physiological and security needs. You don't have much say over what your workers eat or drink, or where they live; neither do you have the authority to provide them with the same security as the company, union or government.

Most people spend more waking hours involved with their jobs than with their families. To meet the level of need Maslow called "social", employees need to feel they are a part of their "work" family. You as the supervisor do have an influence on the social experience as it occurs in the warehouse. You can motivate your workers by creating a positive work environment. This means simply showing them that you care about them as people. Filling the social needs of your employees can be as personal as remembering their birthdays and anniversaries or as simple as assigning new employees a "buddy" for their first day on the job.

The level of need that the supervisor has the most control over is the self-esteem. If an employee loses his self-esteem, I can guarantee that he'll also lose productivity. Egos are very susceptible to self-fulfilling prophecies, both positive and negative. By this I mean that employees tend to perform up — or down — to your expectations. If you convince an order selector that he's stupid, you'll probably wind up with a slow and stupid order selector on your crew. On the other hand, you can build his self-esteem (and

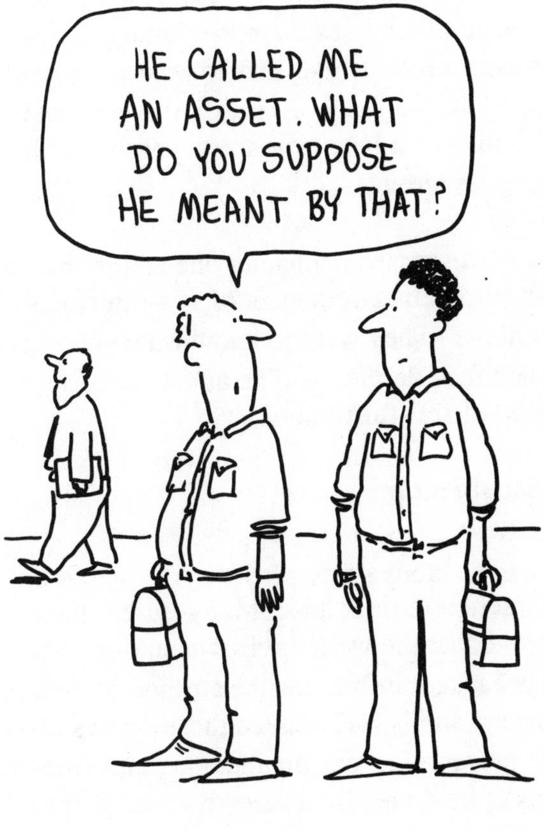
HE CALLED ME AN ASSET. WHAT DO YOU SUPPOSE HE MEANT BY THAT?

consequently, his performance) by listening to his ideas, expressing confidence in his work, and sharing information with him.

All employees want feedback from their boss. They want to know that he feels good about them and the work they do. This recognition gives them the dignity that helps fill the self-esteem need. It's so easy to ignore the worker that does a good job every day. After all, that is what is expected of him. He'll hear from the supervisor only when something goes wrong.

The goals we discussed in chapter one and in this chapter are also an important component of self-esteem. People want to achieve. They want to know what you expect of them. When they do they will be able to experience the highest need of self-fulfillment.

Getting Satisfaction

Another way to motivate employees is to help them find more satisfaction in their jobs. Many studies have been done to prove that the work environment does affect productivity because it influences the attitude of their employees. Herzberg, in his study called these factors dissatisfiers. If they are present they can distract the employee from what needs to be done. Be aware however, that each situation needs to be evaluated separately. A happy employee does not necessarily guarantee a productive employee, but it is safe to say that a majority of employees are influenced by factors of their work environment. Here are some examples of work environment factors that can cause problems:

- Policies. These are the company's values, goals, and methods. When employees don't understand policies, they don't feel like part of the organization, and they make more mistakes.

- Procedures. This area, which includes benefits, vacations, pay scales, and promotions, lies near and dear to every employee. A misunderstanding about procedures can cause a lot of resentment.

- Working Conditions. Unsafe or unsanitary work environments tell employees that management, including the supervisor, doesn't care about their welfare.

Push Button Power

Motivation is basically an "inside job." By this I mean that **people are motivated by a sense of ownership in their work.** No amount of money or vacation time can substitute for job-related motivators, such as feeling proud of your work, participating in decisions that affect your job, and receiving recognition for a job well done. Eliminating job-related problems tends to increase long-term job satisfaction, while correcting work environment problems may or may not make your employees happy.

I once heard a story about a company that encouraged employees to take ownership in their jobs. This corporation, a car manufacturer, operated a factory that contained miles of assembly lines under one roof. In front of every worker, the company installed a push button that could bring the assembly line to a screeching halt.

If you've ever worked on an assembly line — especially in a large manufacturing operation — you'll realize that installing a stop button was a brave action. No matter what else goes wrong, it's essential to keep an assembly line moving. Any delay can cause chain-reaction traffic jams and cost thousands of dollars in damaged parts and lost time. By giving employees the power to control the assembly line, this company demonstrated that each worker was important. The employees never pushed the button, but knowing that they could stop the assembly line gave them a sense of participation in their work.

You don't have to install assembly lines and stop buttons to motivate your employees. Utilizing the following steps can also increase their job satisfaction:

- Give your employees challenging, but achievable, tasks.

- Tell them how their jobs relate to the rest of

the company. Their performance affects the entire organization's performance.

- Give employees as much responsibility as possible, so that they will feel an ownership in their job, and care about the results. The manager of a warehouse with nineteen people told me he delegates to the lowest level possible. In that system, you as a supervisor can benefit in two ways. People feel good when you give them responsibilities and you have more time to devote to managing.

Calling For Reinforcements

As I said earlier, the first line supervisor can encourage good job performance by motivating his employees. Maintaining a high level of performance, however, requires positive reinforcement — a psychology term for techniques that increase the chances of a desired behavior continuing.

Let's say that several trucks arrive unexpectedly during your shift, and all of them need to be unloaded right away. Instead of complaining about the time crunch, the employees on the dock take the situation in stride, clearing the shipping lanes and matching orders to the right truck. You're glad that you don't have to nag them about working fast, but accurately.

When the hurly-burly is over, you approach the three loaders and smile. "You guys worked your tails off just now, and did a good job of it. Thanks a lot." You might give them the rest of the afternoon off. Or, you may offer to buy them a cup of coffee or lunch. Giving your employees rewards such as these will <u>reinforce</u> their performance, increasing the likelihood that your employees will give a repeat performance the next time there's a rush on the loading dock.

Different Strokes

It might be nice if you could motivate and reinforce your workers by treating them all the same. That's not the case, however. Although one employee may want lavish praise for his performance, that might only embarrass his co-worker, who would settle for a pat on the back — or better yet, a new pallet jack. People are motivated by different things, and therefore require different reinforcers. You need to know each of your employees well enough to choose the appropriate reward.

Positive reinforcers tend to fall into one of four general categories: social reinforcers, recognition, feedback, and approval of requests. You use social reinforcers when you praise employees, smile at them, shake their hands, or buy them a cup of coffee. Recognition, a more formal reinforcer, involves letters of commendation, awards ceremonies, and other forms of public praise. **Feedback acts as positive reinforcement because it provides employees** with specific information about their actions, work, and ideas: you're telling them how their work helped the organization, how close they came to achieving a goal, how the company intends to take action on their suggestions. You can also reinforce employee performance by approving their requests for time off, additional training, permission to try a new method, additional help or equipment.

Waiting For Mr. Right

If you don't bother to reinforce your employees, your relationship with your crew will definitely suffer the consequences. I saw this happen in one warehouse, as I talked with one of the employees about a particular method. From where we stood on the loading dock, we could see the first line supervisor coming towards us. The operator nodded at the approaching figure and said under his breath, "There he comes; I wonder what I did wrong now." It seems that the supervisor only talked with the employee about mistakes and problems — never a word of encouragement, praise, or greeting.

Is that the kind of message you're leaving with your employees? Do they dread seeing you approach? If so, you need to catch your employees doing something right, instead of paying so much attention to their mistakes. Here are some additional thoughts to keep in mind when reinforcing your employees' performance:

- Give the positive reinforcement as soon as possible after the desired behavior. In golf, you know immediately whether the swing was good or bad. In the same way, employees need immediate feedback on their performance so that they'll remember exactly what they did right. Praise the employee while he's working, not during his coffee break.

- Link the reinforcement with the desired performance. Positive reinforcement must be intentional. Employees can't read your mind; you have to tell them up front that you're praising them, and why.

- Be specific. For example, if an order selector has the lowest rate of damaged goods in the whole crew, compliment him on the fact, not for "doing a good job."

Putting the Puzzle Together

As a first line supervisor, you may not have control over some motivating and reinforcing tools, such as vacations, time off, pay raises, or performance awards. But you do have the control to show them that you and the company care about their well-being.

Maintaining long-term motivation depends on a positive

work environment. I've been to a lot of sales meetings and heard my share of Norman Vincent Peale-like inspirational speakers. They get people all pumped up to leave the meeting feeling like they've got the world by the tail. It's only a temporary lift, however. Two days later, they're back at work, dealing with the same old problems. In the same way, you can praise one of your employees and motivate him for a day or two, but it won't last forever.

It's the whole environment that encourages and maintains worker performance. Like pieces of a jig-saw puzzle, many separate actions combine to create a positive work environment. This book has covered several pieces of that puzzle: improving communication, removing barriers to productivity, training, setting goals, and encouraging good performance. When you put the puzzle together, it's no longer just a collection of different pieces. It is a whole new picture. These various skills — pieces of the puzzle — also work together to make something new: a first line supervisor.

GLOSSARY

Accountability - The measurement of a supervisor's progress toward meeting management's objectives.

Authority - The right and the power to do what needs to be done to meet the responsibilities.

Communication - An exchange of information that flows in two directions within organizations: downward and upward usually through the supervisor. It can be verbal, non-verbal or written.

Employees - The most valuable, high-priced asset in the warehouse.

Evaluation - To examine or judge the quality of the work according to the standards set. Needs to be done with each employee on a scheduled basis.

Feedback - Part of the communication loop — letting people know how well they did against the set goals.

First Line Supervisor - Key to the warehouse — Part of the management team assigned to managing the human resources that run the warehouse.

Goals - What is expected of the worker to fulfill the priorities of the company. They are measurable and achievable. They will only be met if they are communicated to the employees who will implement them.

Grapevine - The employee source of information when correct information isn't being communicated by the supervisor or manager. A rumor mill that breeds uncertainty, misinformation and resentment.

Hidden Lost Time - Lost time that is not obvious but can add up to a considerable loss when computated.

Job Definition - Understanding the responsibility, accountability and authority that goes with your job.

Listening - One of the most effective ways to create a positive environment in the warehouse — hearing what employees say and acting on what they tell you.

Lost Time - Non-productive time. This can be obvious or hidden.

Management by Objectives - Applying the company's objectives to your own work.

Management by Walking Around - Spending time on the floor, talking with individual employees to facilitate communication as well as motivation.

Measurement - Assigning a method to a task — determined by productivity, utilization and performance.

Performance - The comparison of how long it took to how long it should have taken — actual time versus standard time.

Policies - The values, goals and methods of the company that need to be understood by the employees if they are going to feel a part of the organization.

Positive Work Environment - An environment in which people can work to their capabilities and know that their work makes a difference to the company.

Preventive Maintenance - Removing the source of potential problems before they grow.

Prioritizing - Labelling tasks so that time spent on them is relative to their importance.

Productivity - The ratio of real output to real input.

Productivity Barriers - Problems that set up roadblocks which keep people from attaining the set goals.

Responsibility - The "what" and "why" of a job — understanding management's objectives and expectations. This is to be reviewed and redefined annually.

Scheduling - Planning the time of each day so work doesn't just happen. Keeps lost time to a minimum. Places an expectation on each task.

Scheduled Expectancies - Information you need to set up a work sampling audit.

Self-esteem - The image every person has of themselves and how they fit in. Directly affects productivity.

Utilization - The ratio of capacity used to available capacity.

Working Conditions - The work methods and environment that tell the workers nonverbally how the company, and therefore the supervisor feels about them.

Work Sampling - A daily time log done randomly during a month to track your day. Includes jobs done, as well as events and problems that required your time.

ORDER FORM

Mail your order today for *SUPERVISING ON THE LINE* by Gene Gagnon.

_____ Yes, please send me _____ copies of *SUPERVISING ON THE LINE* for only 12.95 (please enclose payment)

I understand I may return the book for a full refund if not satisfied.

NAME _____

COMPANY _____

ADDRESS _____

CITY _____

STATE _____ ZIP CODE _____

Shipping: $1.00 for the first book and 50¢ for each additional book.

_____ I can't wait 3 - 4 weeks for Book Rate. Enclosed is $3.00 per book for Air Mail.

Thank you for your order and keep a watch for upcoming books by Gene Gagnon and Margo.

Mail to: Margo
P.O. Box 1G
Minnetonka, MN 55345

Notes

Notes

Notes

Notes

Notes

Notes